The Happy England of Helen Allingham

The Happy England of
Helen
Allingham

Marcus B. Huish

with 80 full-colour illustrations by
HELEN ALLINGHAM

Bracken Books
LONDON

Originally published in 1903 as *Happy England* by Adam & Charles Black.

This edition published 1985 by Bracken Books,
a division of Bestseller Publications Ltd,
Brent House, 24 Friern Park, North Finchley,
London N12, England.

ISBN 0 946495 58 0

Printed and bound by Kultura, Hungary.

Contents

CHAPTER I

Page

Our Title 1

CHAPTER II

Paintresses, Past and Present 13

CHAPTER III

The Artist's Early Work 27

CHAPTER IV

The Artist's Surrey Home 67

CHAPTER V

The Influence of Witley 81

CHAPTER VI

The Woods, the Lanes, and the Fields . . . 98

v

CHAPTER VII

Cottages and Homesteads 118

Page

CHAPTER VIII

Gardens and Orchards 151

CHAPTER IX

Tennyson's Homes 168

CHAPTER X

Mrs. Allingham and her Contemporaries . . . 181

List of Illustrations

1. Portrait of the Artist

Between pages 38 and 39

2. In the Farmhouse Garden
3. The Market Cross, Hagbourne
4. The Robin
5. Milton's House, Chalfont St. Giles
6. The Waller Oak, Coleshill
7. Apple and Pear Blossom
8. The Young Customers
9. The Sand-Martin's Haunt
10. The Old Men's Gardens, Chelsea Hospital
11. The Clothes-Line
12. The Convalescent
13. The Goat Carriage
14. The Clothes-Basket
15. In the Hayloft
16. The Rabbit Hutch
17. The Donkey Ride

Between pages 70 and 71

18. A Witley Lane
19. Hindhead from Witley Common
20. In Witley Village
21. Blackdown from Witley Common

HAPPY ENGLAND

22. The Fish-Shop, Haslemere
23. The Children's Tea
24. The Stile
25. "Pat-a-Cake"
26. Lessons
27. Bubbles
28. On the Sands – Sandown, Isle of Wight
29. Drying Clothes
30. Her Majesty's Post Office
31. The Children's Maypole
32. Spring on the Kentish Downs
33. Tig Bridge

Between pages 102 and 103

34. Spring in the Oakwood
35. The Cuckoo
36. The Old Yew Tree
37. The Hawthorn Valley, Brocket
38. Ox-eye Daisies, near Westerham, Kent
39. Foxgloves
40. Heather on Crockham Hill, Kent
41. On the Pilgrim's Way
42. Night-jar Lane, Witley
43. Cherry-tree Cottage, Chiddingfold
44. Cottage at Chiddingfold
45. A Cottage at Hambledon
46. In Wormley Wood
47. The Elder Bush, Brook Lane, Witley
48. The Basket Woman
49. Cottage at Shottermill, near Haslemere

Between pages 134 and 135

50. Valewood Farm
51. An Old House at West Tarring

LIST OF ILLUSTRATIONS

52. An Old Buckinghamshire House

53. Duke's Cottage

54. The Condemned Cottage

55. On Ide Hill

56. A Cheshire Cottage, Alderley Edge

57. The Six Bells

58. A Kentish Farmyard

59. Study of a Rose Bush

60. Wallflowers

61. Minna

62. A Kentish Garden

63. Cutting Cabbages

64. In A Summer Garden

65. By the Terrace, Brocket Hall

Between pages 166 and 167

66. The South Border

67. The South Border

68. Study of Leeks

69. The Apple Orchard

70. The House, Farringford

71. The Kitchen-Garden, Farringford

72. The Dairy, Farringford

73. One of Lord Tennyson's Cottages, Farringford

74. A Garden in October, Aldworth

75. Hook Hill Farm, Freshwater

76. At Pound Green, Freshwater, Isle of Wight

77. A Cottage at Freshwater Gate

78. A Cabin at Ballyshannon

79. The Fairy Bridges

80. The Church of Sta. Maria Della Salute, Venice

81. A Fruit Stall, Venice

Fradelle & Young.

Happy England

CHAPTER I

OUR TITLE

To choose a title that will felicitously fit the life-work of an artist is no easy matter, especially when the product is a very varied one, and the producer is disposed to take a modest estimate of its value.

In the present case the titles that have suggested themselves to one or other of those concerned in the selection have not been few, and a friendly contest has ensued over the desire of the artist on the one hand to belittle, and of author and publishers on the other to fairly appraise, both the ground which her work covers and the qualities which it contains.

The first point to be considered in giving the

volume a name was that it forms one of a series
in which an endeavour—and, to judge by public
appreciation, a successful endeavour—has been
made to illustrate in colour an artist's impressions
of a particular country : as, for instance, Mr. John
Fulleylove's of the Holy Land, Mr. Talbot Kelly's
of Egypt, and Mr. Mortimer Menpes's of Japan.
Now Mrs. Allingham throughout her work has
been steadfast in her adherence to the portrayal
of one country only.   She has never travelled or
painted outside Europe, and within its limits only
at one place outside the British Isles, namely,
Venice.   Even in her native country her work
has been strictly localised.   Neither Scotland nor
Wales has attracted her attention since the days
when she first worked seriously as an artist, and
Ireland has only received a scanty meed, and that
due to family ties.   England, therefore, was the
one and only name under which her work could
be included within the series, and that has very
properly been assigned to it.

But it will be seen that to this has been added
the prefix "Happy," thereby drawing down the
disapprobation of certain of the artist's friends,
who, recognising her as a resident in Hampstead,
have associated the title with that alliterative one

which the northern suburbs have received at the hands of the Bank Holiday visitant; and they facetiously surmise that the work may be called "'Appy England! By a Denizen of 'Appy 'Ampstead!"

But a glance at the illustrations by any one unacquainted with Mrs. Allingham's residential qualifications, and by the still greater number ignorant even of her name (for these, in spite of her well-earned reputation, will be the majority, taking the countries over which this volume will circulate), must convince such an one that the "England" requires and deserves not only a qualifying but a commendatory prefix, and that the best that will fit it is that to which the artist has now submitted.

We say a "qualifying" title, because within its covers we find only a one-sided and partial view of both life and landscape. None of the sterner realities of either are presented. In strong opposition to the tendency of the art of the later years of the nineteenth century, the baser side of life has been studiously avoided, and nature has only been put down on paper in its happiest moods and its pleasantest array. Storm and stress in both life and landscape are altogether absent.

We say, further, a "commendatory" title, because
as regards both life and landscape it is, throughout,
a mirror of halcyon days. If sickness intrudes on
a single occasion, it is in its convalescent stage;
if old age, it is in a "Haven of Rest"; the wandering pedlar finds a ready market for her wares, the
tramp assistance by the wayside. In both life and
landscape it is a portrayal of youth rejoicing in
its youth. For the most part it represents childhood, and, if we are to believe Mr. Ruskin, for the
first time in modern Art; for in his lecture on Mrs.
Allingham at Oxford, he declared that "though
long by academic art denied or resisted, at last
bursting out like one of the sweet Surrey foun-
tains, all dazzling and pure, you have the radiance
and innocence of reinstated infant divinity showered
again among the flowers of English meadows of
Mrs. Allingham."

This healthiness, happiness, and joy of life,
coupled with an idyllic beauty, reveals itself in
every figure in Mrs. Allingham's story, so that
even the drudgery of rural life is made to appear
as a task to be envied.

And the same joyous and happy note is to be
found in her landscapes. Every scene is

Full in the smile of the blue firmament.

One feels that

> Every flower
> Enjoys the air it breathes.

Rain, wind, or lowering skies find no place in any of them, but each calls forth the expression

> What a day
> To sun one and do nothing!

No attempt is made to select the sterner effects of landscape which earlier English painters so persistently affected. With the rough steeps of Hindhead at her door, the artist's feet have almost invariably turned towards the lowlands and the reposeful forms of the distant South Downs. Cottages, farmsteads, and flower gardens have been her choice in preference to dales, crags, and fells.

And in so selecting, and so delineating, she has certainly catered for the happiness of the greater number.

What does the worker, long in city pent, desire when he cries

> 'Tis very sweet to look into the fair
> And open face of heaven?

And what does the banished Englishman oftenest turn his thoughts to, even although he may be dwelling under aspects of nature which many would think far more beautiful than those of his native land?   Browning in his "Home Thoughts from Abroad" gives consummate expression to the homesickness of many an exile :—

> Oh! to be in England
> Now that April's there!
>
> .   .   .   .   .   .
>
> All will be gay when noontide wakes anew
> The Buttercups, the little children's dower,
> Far brighter than this gaudy melon flower!

And Keats also—

> Happy is England!   I could be content
> To see no other verdure than its own,
> To feel no other breezes than are blown
> Through its tall woods, with high romances blent.

These, the poets' longings, suggested the prefix for which so lengthy an apology has been made, and which, in spite of the artist's demur, we have pressed upon her acceptance, confident that the public verdict will be an acquittal against any charge either of exaggeration, or that he who excuses himself accuses himself.

If an apology is due it is in respect of the letterpress.   The necessity of maintaining the size to which the public has been accustomed in the series of which this forms a part, and of interleaving the numerous illustrations which it contains, means the provision of a certain number of words. Now an artist's life that has been passed amid such pleasant surroundings as has that of Mrs. Allingham, cannot contain a sufficiency of material for the purpose. Indulgence must, therefore, be granted when it is found that much of the contents consists merely of the writer's descriptions of the illustrations, a discovery which might suggest that they were primarily the *raison d'être* of the volume.

As regards the illustrations, a word must be said.

The remarkable achievements in colour reproduction, through what is known as the "three-colour process," have enabled the public to be placed in possession of memorials of an artist's work in a way that was not possible even so recently as a year or two ago. Hitherto self-respecting painters have very rightly demurred to any colour reproductions of their work being made except by processes whose cost and lengthy procedure prohibited quantity as well as quality. Mrs. Allingham herself, in view of previous attempts, was of the same opinion until a trial of the process now adopted convinced her to the

contrary. Now she is happy that a leap forward
in science has enabled renderings in little of her
water-colours to be offered to thousands who did
not know them previously.

2. IN THE FARMHOUSE GARDEN

From the Water-colour in the possession of the Artist.

Painted 1903.

A PORTRAIT of Vi, the daughter of the farmer at whose house in Kent Mrs. Allingham stays.

Mrs. Allingham was tempted to take up again her disused practice of portrait-painting, by the attraction of the combination of the yellow of the child's hair and hat, the red of the roses, and the blue of the distant hillside.

3. THE MARKET CROSS, HAGBOURNE

From the Water-colour in the possession of Mrs. E. Lamb.

Painted 1898.

Berkshire, in spite of its notable places and situation, does not boast of much in the way of county chronicles, and little can be learnt by one whose sole resource is a Murray's *Guide* concerning the interesting village where the scene of this drawing is laid, for it is there dismissed in a couple of lines.

Hagbourne, or Hagborne, is one of the many

"bornes" which (in the counties bordering on the Thames, as elsewhere) takes its Saxon affix from one of the burns or brooks which find their way from thence into the neighbouring river. It lies off the Great Western main line, and its fine church may be seen a mile away to the southward just before arriving at Didcot. This proximity to a considerable railway junction has not disturbed much of its old-world character.

The buildings and the Cross, which make a delightful harmony in greys, probably looked much the same when Cavalier and Puritan harried this district in the Civil War, for with Newbury on one side and Oxford on the other, they must oftentimes have been up and down this, the main street of the village. The Cross has long since lost its meaning. The folk from the countryside no longer bring their butter, eggs, and farm produce for local sale. The villagers have to be content with margarine, French eggs, and other foreign commodities from the local "stores," and the Cross steps are now only of use for infant energies to practise their powers of jumping from. So, too, the sun-dial on the top, which does not appear to have ever been surmounted by a cross, is now useless, for everybody either has a watch or is sufficiently notified as to

meal times by a "buzzer" at the railway works
hard by.

Mrs. Allingham says that most of her drawings
are marked in her memory by some local comment
concerning them. In this case a bystander sym-
pathetically remarked that it seemed "a mighty
tedious job," in that of "Milton's House" that "it
was a foolish little thing when you began"—the
most favourable criticism she ever encountered only
amounting to "Why, it's almost worth framing!"

4. THE ROBIN

From the Water-colour in the possession of Mr. S. H. S. Lofthouse.

Painted 1898.

One of the simplest, and yet one of the most
satisfying of Mrs. Allingham's compositions.

It is clearly not a morning to stay indoors with
needlework which neither in size nor importance
calls for table or chair. Besides, at the cottage
gate there is a likelier chance of interruption and
conversation with occasional passers-by. But, at
no time numerous on this Surrey hillside, these are
altogether lacking at the moment, and the pink-
frocked maiden has to be content with the very

mild distraction afforded by the overtures of the family robin, who is always ready to open up converse and to waste his time also in manœuvres and pretended explorations over ground in her vicinity, which he well knows to be altogether barren of provender.

CHAPTER II

Man took advantage of his strength to be
First in the field : some ages have been lost;
But woman ripens earlier, and her life is longer—
Let her not fear.

THE fair sex is so much in evidence in Art to-day
(the first census of this century recording the names
of nearly four thousand who profess that calling)
that we are apt to forget that the lady artist,
worthy of a place amongst the foremost of the
other sex, is a creation of modern growth.

Paintresses—to call them by a quaint and agreeable name—there have been in profusion, and an
author, writing a quarter of a century ago, managed
to fill two bulky volumes[1] with their biographies ;
but the majority of these have owed both their
practice and their place in Art to the fact of their

[1] Clayton's *English Female Artists,* 1876.

13

fathers or husbands having been engaged in that profession.

History has recorded but little concerning the women artists who worked in the early days of English Art. The scanty records which, however, have come down to us prove that if they lived uneventful lives they did so in comfort. For instance, it is noted of the first that passes across the pages of English history, namely Susannah Hornebolt (all the early names were foreign), that she lived for many years in great favour and esteem at the King's Court, and died rich and honoured: of the next, Lavinia Teerlinck, that she also died rich and respected, having received in her prime a higher salary than Holbein, and from Queen Elizabeth, later on in life, a quarterly wage of £41. Farther on we find Charles I. giving to Anne Carlisle and Vandyck, at one time, as much ultramarine as cost him £500, and Anna Maria Carew obtaining from Charles II. in 1662 a pension of £200 a year. About the same time Mary Beale, who is described as passing a tranquil, modest existence, full of sweetness, dignity, and matronly purity, earned the same amount from her brush, charging £5 for a head, and £10 for a half-length. She died in 1697, and was buried under the communion table in St. James's, Piccadilly, a church which holds the remains of other paintresses.

Another, Mary Delaney, described as "lovely in girlhood and old age," and who must have been a delightful personage from the testimonies which have come down to us concerning her, lived almost through the eighteenth century, being born in 1700, and dying in 1788, and being, also, buried in St. James's. She has left on record that " I have been very busy at my usual presumption of copying beautiful nature"; but the many copies of that kind that she must have made during this long life are all unknown to those who have studied Art a hundred years later.

Midway in the eighteenth century we come across the great and unique event in the annals of Female Art, namely the election of two ladies to the Academic body, in the persons of Angelica Kauffman—who was one of the original signatories of the memorial to George III., asking him to found an Academy, and who passed in as such on the granting of that privilege—and Mary Moser, who probably owed her election to the fact that her father was Keeper of the newly-founded body.

The only other lady artists who flit across the stage during the latter half of that century—in the

case of whom any attempt at distinction or recognition is possible—were Frances Reynolds, the
sister of the President, and the "dearest dear" of
Dr. Johnson, and Maria Cosway, the wife of the
miniaturist. These kept up the tradition of ladies
always being connected with Art by parentage or
marriage.

The Academy catalogues of the first half of the
nineteenth century may be searched in vain for
any name whose fame has endured even to these
times, although the number of lady exhibitors was
considerable. In the exhibitions of fifty years ago,
of 900 names, 67, or 7 per cent, were those of the
fair sex, the majority being termed in the alpha-
betical list " Mrs. ——, as above "; that is to say,
they bore the surname and lived at the same
addresses as the exhibitor who preceded them.[1]

The admission of women to the Royal Academy
Schools in 1860 must not only have had much to do
with increasing the numbers of paintresses, but in
raising the standard of their work. In recent years,
at the annual prize distributions of that institution,
when they present themselves in such interesting
and serried ranks, they have firmly established their

[1] In the Exhibition of 1903, 330 out of 1180, or 28 per cent, were
ladies.

right to work alongside of the men, by carrying off many of the most important awards.[1]

The Royal Female School of Art, the Slade School, and Schools of Art everywhere throughout the country each and all are now engaged in swelling the ranks of the profession with a far greater number of aspirants to a living than there is any room for.

This invasion of womankind into Art, which has also shown itself in a remarkable way in poetry and fiction, is in no way to be decried. On the contrary, it has come upon the present generation as a delightful surprise, as a breath of fresh and sweet-scented air after the heavy atmosphere which hung over Art in the later days of the nineteenth century.   To mention a few only: Miss Elizabeth Thompson (Lady Butler), Lady Alma Tadema, Mrs. Jopling, Miss Dicksee, Mrs. Henrietta Rae, Miss Kemp Welch, and Miss Brickdale in oil painting ; Mrs. Angell, Miss Clara Montalba, Miss Gow, Miss Kate Greenaway, and Mrs. Allingham in water-colours have each looked at Art in a distinguished manner, and one quite

---

[1] The first female gold medallist was Miss Louisa Starr (now Madame Canziani), and she was followed by Miss Jessie Macgregor, a niece of Alfred Hunt.

distinct from that of their fellow-workers of the sterner sex.

The ladies named all entered upon their profession with a due sense of its importance. Many of them may perhaps be counted fortunate in having commenced their careers before the newer ideas came into vogue, by virtue of which anybody and everybody may pose as an artist, now that it entails none of that lengthy apprenticeship which from all time has been deemed to be a necessary preliminary to practice. Even so lately as the date when Mrs. Allingham came upon the scene, draftsmanship and composition were still regarded as a matter of some importance if success was to be achieved. Nature, as represented in Art, was still subjected to a process of selection, a selection, too, of its higher in preference to its lower forms. The same pattern was not allowed to serve for every tree in the landscape whatever be its growth, foliage, or the local influences which have affected its form. A sufficient study of the human and of animal forms to admit of their introduction, if needful, into that landscape was not deemed superfluous. Most important of all, beauty still held the field, and the cult of unvarnished ugliness had not captured the rising generation.

The endeavours of women in what is termed very erroneously the higher branch of the profession, have not as yet received the reward that is their due. Placed at the Royal Academy under practically the same conditions as the male sex whilst under tuition, both as regards fortune and success, their pictures, when they mount from the Schools in the basement to the Exhibition Galleries on the first floor of Burlington House, carry with them no further possibility of reward, even although, as they have done, they hold the pride of place there. It is true that as each election to the Academic body comes round rumours arise as to the chances of one or other of the fair sex forcing an entrance through the doors that, with the two exceptions we have named, have been barred to them since the foundation of the Institution. The day, however, when their talent in oil painting, or any other art medium, will be recognised by Academic honours has yet to come.

To their honour be it said, the undoubted capacities of ladies have not passed unrecognised by water-colour painters. Both the Royal Society and the Royal Institute of Painters in Water Colours have enrolled amongst their ranks the names of women who have been worthy exponents of the Art.

The practice of water-colour art would appear
to appeal especially to womankind, as not only
are the constituents which go to its making of
a more agreeable character than those of oil, but
the whole machinery necessary for its successful
production is more compact and capable of adaptation to the ordinary house. The very methods
employed have a certain daintiness about them
which coincides with a lady's delicacy. The work
does not necessitate hours of standing, with evil-
smelling paints, in a large top-lit studio, but can be
effected seated, in any living room which contains
a window of sufficient size. There is no need to
leave all the materials about while the canvasses
dry, and no preliminary setting of palettes and
subsequent cleaning off.

Yet in spite of this the water-colour art during
the first century of its existence was practised
almost solely by the male sex, and it was not until
the middle of the Victorian reign that a few women
came on to the scene, and at once showed themselves the equals of the male sex, not only so far
as proficiency but originality was concerned. In
the case of no one of these was there any imitation
or following of a master; but each struck out for
herself what was, if not a new line, certainly a

presentation of an old one in a novel form.   Mrs.
Angell, better known perhaps as Helen Coleman,
took up the portrayal of flowers and still life, which
had been carried to such a pitch of minute finish
by William Hunt, and treated it with a breadth,
freedom, and freshness that delighted everybody.
It secured for her at once a place amid a section
of water-colourists who found it very difficult to
obtain these qualities in their work.   Miss Clara
Montalba went to Venice and painted it under
aspects which were entirely different from those of
her predecessors, such as James Holland; and she
again has practically held the field ever since as
regards that particular phase of atmospheric effect
which has attracted attention to her achievement.
The kind of work and the subjects taken up by
Mrs. Allingham will be dealt with at greater length
hereafter, but I may premise by saying that she,
too, ultimately settled into methods that are entirely her own, and such as no one can accuse her
of having derived from anybody else.

———————

THE following illustrations find a place in this
chapter :—

5. MILTON'S HOUSE, CHALFONT ST. GILES

From the Water-colour in the possession of Mrs. J. A. Combe

Painted 1898.

THE popularity of a poet can hardly be gauged by the number of visitors to the haunts wherein he passed his day. Rather are they numbered by the proximity of a railroad thereto. Consequently it is not surprising that the pilgrims to the little out-of-the-way Buckinghamshire village where Milton completed his *Paradise Lost* are an inconsiderable percentage of those who journey to Stratford-on-Avon. For though Chalfont St. Giles lies only a short distance away from the twenty-third milestone on the high-road from London to Aylesbury, it is some three miles from the nearest station—a station, too, where few conveyances are obtainable. Motor cars which will take the would-be pilgrim in an hour from a Northumberland Avenue hotel may increase its popularity, but at present the village of the "pretty box," as Milton called the house, is as slumberous and as little changed as it was in the year 1665, when Milton fled thither from his house in Artillery Ground, Bunhill Row,

before the terror of the plague.[1]   Milton was then
fifty-seven, and is described as a pale, but not
cadaverous man, dressed neatly in black, with his
hands and fingers gouty, and with chalk-stones.
He loved a garden, and would never take a house,
not even in London, without one, his habit being
to sit in the sun in his garden, or in the colder
weather to pace it for three or four hours at a
stretch.   Many of his verses he composed or pruned
as he thus walked, coming in to dictate them to his
amanuensis, and it was from the vernal to the
autumnal equinox that his intermittent inspiration
bore its fruit.   His only other recreation besides
conversation was music, and he sang, and played
either the organ or the bass viol.   It was at
Chalfont that Milton put into the hands of
Ellwood his completed *Paradise Lost*, with a
request that he would return it to him with his
judgment thereupon.   It was here also that on
receiving Ellwood's famous opinion, "Thou hast
said much here of Paradise Lost, but what hast
thou to say of Paradise Found?" he commenced his *Paradise Regained.*   He returned to
London after the plague abated, in time to see

[1] The Parish Register shows that the plague reached Chalfont
later on.

it again devastated by the fresh calamity of the great fire.

An engraving of this house appears in Dunster's edition of *Paradise Regained*, and an account in Todd's *Life of Milton*, p. 272; also in Jesse's *Favourite Haunts*, p. 62.

6. THE WALLER OAK, COLESHILL

From the Water-colour in the possession of the Artist.

Painted 1902.

That several of Mrs. Allingham's drawings should illustrate scenes connected with Great Britain's poets is not remarkable, seeing that her life has been so intimately bound up with one of them, but it is at first somewhat startling to find that the two selected for illustration here should treat of Milton and Waller, for was it not the latter who said of *Paradise Lost* that it was distinguished only by its length. The accident that has brought them together here is perhaps that the two scenes are near neighbours, and, may be, the artist was tempted to paint the old oak through kindly sentiments towards the author of the sweet-smelling lines, "Go, Lovely Rose," by which his name endures.

Coleshill, where the oak stands, is a "woody hamlet" near Amersham, and a mile or two away from Chalfont St. Giles. The tree which bears his name, and under which he is said to have composed much of his verse, dates from long anterior to the late days of the Monarchy, when he was more engaged in hatching plots than in writing verse. If, as is probable, he viewed and sought its comforting shade, he can hardly have believed that it would survive the fame of him who received such praise from his contemporaries as to be acclaimed "inter poetas sui temporis facile princeps."

7. APPLE AND PEAR BLOSSOM

From the Water-colour in the possession of Mr. Theodore Uzielli.

Painted 1901.

A charming little picture made out of the simplest details is this spring scene in an Isle of Wight lane. But if the details are of the simplest character, as much cannot be said for the methods employed by the artist in their treatment. These

are so intricate that the drawing was perhaps the
most difficult of any to reproduce, owing to the
impossibility of accurately translating the subtle
gradations which distinguish the tender greenery
of trees, hedgerow, and bank.

CHAPTER III

THE ARTIST'S EARLY WORK

Mrs. Allingham, whose maiden name was Helen Paterson, was born on September 26, 1848, near Burton-on-Trent, Derbyshire, where her father, Alexander Henry Paterson, M.D., had a medical practice. As her name implies, she is of Scottish descent on the paternal side. A year after her birth her family removed to Altrincham in Cheshire, where her father died suddenly, in 1862, of diphtheria, caught in attending a patient.

This unforeseen blow broke up the Cheshire household, and the widow shortly afterwards wended her way with her young family to Birmingham, where the next few years, the most impressionable of our young artist's life, were to be spent amid surroundings which at that date were in no wise conducive to influencing her in the direction of Art of any kind.

27

Scribbling out of her head on any material she could lay hold of (not even sparing the polished surfaces of the Victorian furniture) had been her chief pleasure as a child ; and as she grew older she drew from Nature with interest and ease, especially during family visits to Kenilworth and other country and seaside places. Some friends in Birmingham started a drawing club which met each month at houses of the different members, and the young student was kindly invited to join it. Subjects were fixed upon and the drawings were shown and discussed at each meeting. More good resulted from this than might have been expected, for some of the members were not only persons of taste but were collectors of fine examples in Art, which were also seen and considered at the meetings. Helen Paterson, finding that her pen-and-ink productions were more satisfactory than her colour attempts, came to hope that she might gradually qualify herself for book illustration, instead of earning a living by teaching, as she at first anticipated her future would be.

Two influences greatly helped the girl in her artistic desires at this time.

Helen Paterson's mother's sister, Laura Herford, had taken up Art as a profession. Although her name does not often appear in Exhibition records, the sisterhood of artists owe her a very enduring debt. For to her was due that opening of the Royal Academy Schools to women to which I have already referred, and which she obtained through another's slip of the tongue, aided by a successful subterfuge.

Lord Lyndhurst, at a Royal Academy banquet, in singing the praises of that institution, claimed that its schools offered free tuition to *all* Her Majesty's subjects. Within a few days he received from Miss Herford a communication pointing out the inaccuracy of his statement, inasmuch as tuition was only given to the male and not to the female sex, which comprised the majority of Her Majesty's subjects. She therefore appealed to him to use his influence with the Government to obtain the removal of the restriction. He did so, and the Government, on addressing Sir Charles Eastlake, the President of the Royal Academy, found in him one altogether in sympathy with such a reform. He replied to the Government that there was no *written* law against the admission of women, and after an interview with the lady he connived at a drawing of hers being sent in as a test of her capability for admission as a probationer, under the

initials merely of her Christian names. A few days
subsequently a notification that he had passed the
test and obtained admission arrived at her home
addressed to A. L. Herford, Esq. There was of
course a demonstration when the lady presented
herself in answer to the summons to execute a
drawing in the presence of the Keeper; and her
claim to stay and do this was vehemently com-
bated by the Council, to whom it was of course
referred. But the President demonstrated the
absurdity of the situation, and so strongly advo-
cated the untenability of the position that the
door was opened once and for all to female
students. This lady, who had a strong character
in many other directions, constituted herself Art-
adviser-in-chief to her young niece from the time
of her father's death.

The other influence under which Helen Paterson came at this critical period was that of a
capable and sympathetic master at Birmingham.
In Mr. Raimbach, the head of the Birmingham
School of Design, she encountered a man who was
a teacher, born not made, and who, not being
hidebound with the old dry-as-dust traditions, saw
and fostered whatever gifts were to be found in his
pupils. He it was who, interesting himself in her

desire to learn to draw the human figure, and to study more of its anatomy than could be gained from the casts of the School of Design and from the lifeless programme which existed there, encouraged her to go to London for wider study, in the hope of gaining entrance into the Academy Schools, and taking up Art as a profession under her aunt's auspices.

She followed his advice, gave up a single pupil she had acquired, and passed into the Academy Schools in April 1867 after a short preliminary course at the Female School of Art, Queen's Square.

British Art may congratulate itself that in Helen Paterson's case, as in that of so many others, "there's a divinity that shapes our ends, rough-hew them how we will." It is very certain that had the fates ordained that she should remain in Birmingham her talent would never have flowed into the channel which has made possible a memoir of her Art under the title of "Happy England." The environments of that great city are such that it would have been practically impossible for her artistic training to have been as her divinity decreed it should be, or to place means of exercising it within her grasp should she have desired them.

During the first year or two at the Royal
Academy Helen Paterson worked in the antique
school, where the study of drawing, proportion
of the figure, with some anatomy, precluded the
thought of painting. When raised to the painting
school she, like many another capable student
then as now, was at first driven hither and thither
by the variety of and apparently contradictory
advice that she received from her masters. For
one month she was under a visitor with strongly
defined ideas in one direction, and the next under
some one else who was equally assertive in another,
and it was some time before she could strike
a balance for her own understanding. But, for
reasons which those who know her well will recognise, she received help and kindness from all, and,
as she gratefully remembers, from none more than
from Millais, Frederick Leighton, Frederick Good-
all, Fred Walker, Stacy Marks, and John Pettie.
Millais especially could in a minute or two impart
something which was never afterwards forgotten,
whilst the encouragement of all was most stimulat-
ing to a beginner. Another artist who has been a
life-long adviser and the kindest of friends, was
Briton Riviere, with whom and whose family an
intimacy began even in her student days. An

invitation to stay with them at St. Andrews on
the coast of Fife in the summer of 1872 in-
augurated Miss Paterson's first serious work from
Nature. The result was deemed to be satisfactory
by Mr. Riviere, who helped to dissipate a certain
despondency and fear which had sprung up in
the young artist's mind as regards her colour
powers. It was not, however, in the grey houses
and uninteresting streets of this old northern uni-
versity town, to which she first turned, that the
true relations between tone and colour discovered
themselves to her longing eye, but amongst the
sandbanks, seaweed, and blue water which fringe
its noted golf-links. For the first time the artist
felt herself happy in attempting to work in any
other medium than black and white. Just prior
to this fortunate visit she had in the spring of the
year been taken by an old friend of the family to
Rome, where she had worked assiduously at Nature,
but with little satisfaction so far as she herself was
concerned.

She had by this time fully made up her mind to
embark on a career in which she was determined,
and was in fact obliged, to earn a living ; and as her
colour work at present had no market, there was
nothing for it but to procure a livelihood by black

and white.　Wood engraving, although nearing the end of its existence, was still the only medium of cheap illustration.　Photography later on came to its aid to a certain extent, but the majority of the original drawings continued to be drawn directly on to the wood block.　There were still close upon a hundred wood engravers employed in London, working for the most part under master engravers, into whose hands the publishers of magazines, illustrated periodicals, and books entrusted, not only the cutting of the block, but the selection of the artist to make the drawing upon it.

It was to these that Helen Paterson had to look for work, and it was upon a round of their offices that in the autumn of 1869 she diffidently started with a portfolio full of drawings.　Employment did not come at once, and the list of seventy names with which she started had been considerably reduced before, to her great satisfaction, a drawing out of her sheaf was taken by Mr. Joseph Swain, to whom she had an introduction, for submission to the proprietors of *Once a Week*.　It was accepted, and she copied it on to the wood. Gradually she obtained work for other magazines, including *Little Folks*, published by Cassell, and *Aunt Judy*, by George Bell, the drawings for

Aunt Judy illustrating Mrs. Ewing's *A Flat Iron for a Farthing, Jan of the Windmill*, and *Six to Sixteen*.

The first alteration of any magnitude of the custom to which reference has been made, namely, of the artist having to look to the engraver for work, occurred when the *Graphic* newspaper was started in the year 1870. Mr. W. L. Thomas, to whom the credit of this improvement in the status of the worker in black and white was due, was himself an artist and a member of the Institute of Painters in Water Colours. As such he was not only in touch with, but capable of appreciating the unusual amount of budding talent of abundant promise which was just then presenting itself. This he enlisted in the service of the *Graphic* upon what may be termed co-operative terms, for those who liked could have half their payment in cash and half in shares in the venture. Many, the majority we believe, unfortunately could not afford the latter proposition. Unfortunately indeed, for the paper embarked on a career which has yielded dividends, at times of over a hundred per cent, and has kept the shares at a premium, which few companies in existence can boast of. This phenomenal success was in a large measure the result of the personal interest that was brought to bear upon every department, and that every employé took in his share in it. The illustrations, upon which success mainly depended, were not the product of a formulated system, working in a groove, where blocks were served out to artists as to a machine, without any regard to their fitness for the particular piece of work. Artists of capacity, whose names are now to be found amongst the most noted in the academic roll, were selected for the particular illustration that suited them, and were well paid for it. The public was not only astonished at, but grateful for, the result, and showed their appreciation by at once placing the *Graphic* in the high position which it deserved and has since enjoyed.

Helen Paterson was so fortunate as to be brought into touch with Mr. Thomas shortly after the first appearance of the paper. She had obtained some work from one Harrall, an engraver, with whom Mr. Thomas had had business connections in the past, and it was at Harrall's suggestion that she went to Mr. Thomas, who at once offered her a place on the staff of the *Graphic*, a place which she retained until her marriage in 1874. It was indeed a godsend to her, for it meant not only

regular work but handsome pay.   Twelve guineas
for a full, and eight for a half page, and at least one
of these a week, meant not merely maintenance,
but a reserve against that rainy day which, fortunately, the subject of our memoir has never had to
contend with.

The subjects which Miss Paterson was called
upon to produce were of the most diversified character, but all of them had figures as their main
feature.   To properly limn these she had to
employ regular models, but she also enlisted the
aid of her fellow-students, for she was still at the
Royal Academy, and her sketch-books of that
time, of which she has many, are full of studies
of artists, no few of whom have since become
celebrated in the world of Art.

Looking through the pages of the *Graphic* with
the artist, it is interesting to note the variety of
episodes upon which Mr. Thomas employed her.
Her drawings were not always from her own
sketches, being at times from originals that had
been sent to the paper in an embryo condition
necessitating entire revision, or from rapid notes
by artists sent to represent the paper at important
functions.   But on occasions she was also deputed
to attend at these, and in consequence underwent

some novel experiences for a young girl.   A meeting at Mr. Gladstone's, Fashions in the Park, Flower Shows at the Botanical Gardens, Archery at the Toxophilite Society's,—these formed the lighter side of her work, the more serious being the illustration of novels by novelists of note.   This was at the time a new feature in journalism.   Amongst those entrusted to her were *Innocent*, by Mrs. Oliphant, and *Ninety-Three*, by Victor Hugo.   For the murder trial in the former she had to visit the Central Criminal Court, and through so doing was more accurate than the authoress, who admittedly had not been there, and whose work consequently showed several glaring mistakes, such as the prisoner addressing the judge by name.   She was also employed upon a novel of Charles Reade's in conjunction with Mr. Luke Fildes and Mr. Henry Woods.   This she undertook with extreme diffidence, for Reade had sent round a circular saying that he greatly disliked having his stories illustrated at all ; but as it had to be in this case, he begged to notify that *he* gave *situations*, whilst George Eliot and Anthony Trollope only gave conversations, and he requested that good use should be made of these situations.   Meeting him some years afterwards, the author paid her the compliment of

2. IN THE FARMHOUSE GARDEN

3. THE MARKET CROSS, HAGBOURNE

4. THE ROBIN

5. MILTON'S HOUSE, CHALFONT ST. GILES

6. THE WALLER OAK, COLESHILL

7. APPLE AND PEAR BLOSSOM

8. THE YOUNG CUSTOMERS

9. THE SAND-MARTIN'S HAUNT

10. THE OLD MEN'S GARDENS, CHELSEA HOSPITAL

11. THE CLOTHES-LINE

12. THE CONVALESCENT

13. THE GOAT CARRIAGE

14. THE CLOTHES-BASKET

15. IN THE HAYLOFT

16. THE RABBIT HUTCH

17. THE DONKEY RIDE

saying he liked her illustration of the heroine in his story the best of any.

Nor was Miss Paterson entirely dependent upon the *Graphic*, whose illustrations, oftentimes given out in a hurry, had to be finished within a period limited by hours. She was fortunate to be numbered amongst the select few who worked for the *Cornhill*, for which she was, through Mr. Swain's kind offices, asked to illustrate Hardy's *Far from the Madding Crowd*, which was at first attributed to George Eliot. The author was fairly complimentary as to the result, although he said it was difficult for two minds to imagine scenes in the same light. Later on she had the pleasant task of illustrating Miss Thackeray's *Miss Angel* in the same magazine. The drawing of Sir Joshua Reynolds asking Angelica to marry him, perhaps the best of the series, was one of the first to be signed with the name of Allingham, by which she has since been known.

A very interesting acquaintance with Sir Henry Irving, which has lasted ever since, was commenced in the early seventies through her having to visit the Lyceum for the *Graphic* to delineate him and Miss Isabel Bateman in *Richelieu*. Mr. Bateman, who was then the manager, placed a box at her disposal, which she occupied for several nights whilst making the drawing. One of the cottage drawings reproduced here (Plate 77) belongs to Sir Henry.

Although working regularly and almost continuously at black and white during these years she managed to intersperse it with some work in colour, and at the exhibitions of the old Dudley Gallery Art Society, which had been recently founded, and which had proved a great boon to rising and amateur art, she exhibited water-colours under the title of "May," "Dangerous Ground," and " Soldiers' Orphans watching a blood-less battle at Aldershot," painted in the studio from a *Graphic* drawing.

In the autumn of the year 1874 Miss Paterson was married to Mr. William Allingham, the well-known poet, editor of *Fraser's Magazine*, and friend of so many of the celebrities in literature, science, and art of the middle of the last century, amongst whom may be mentioned Carlyle, Ruskin, Dante Gabriel Rossetti, Browning, and Tennyson. It was to be near the first named that the newly married couple went to reside in Trafalgar Square, Chelsea, where they passed the next seven years of their married life, namely until 1881.

To Carlyle Mrs. Allingham had the privilege of
frequent and familiar access during his last years ;
and when he found that he was not expected to
pose to her, and that she had, as he emphatically
declared, a real talent for portraiture (the only form
of pictorial art in which he took any interest), he
became very kind and complaisant, and she was able
to make nearly a dozen portraits of him in water-
colours.   An early one, which he declared made him
"look like an old fool," was painted in the little
back garden of No. 5 Cheyne Row, which was not
without shade and greenery in the summer time.
There, in company with his pet cat "Tib," and a
Paisley churchwarden ("no pipe good for anything," according to him, "being get-at-able in
England"), he indulged in smoking, the only
creature comfort that afforded him any satisfaction.   In these portraits he is depicted sitting in
his comfortable dressing-gown faded to a dim slaty
grey, refusing to wear a gorgeous oriental garment
that his admirers had presented to him.   An
etching of one of these drawings appeared in the
Art Journal for 1882.   Other portraits were
painted in the winter of 1878-79, in his long
drawing-room with its three windows looking out
into the street.

Rossetti she never saw, although he had been an intimate friend of her husband's for twenty years[1] and was then living in Chelsea, for he was just entering on that unfortunate epoch preceding his death, when he was induced to cut himself adrift from all his old circle of acquaintances. The fact is regrettable, for it would have been interesting to note his opinion of a lady's work with which he must have been in full sympathy.

Mr. Allingham had known Ruskin for many years. His wife's acquaintance began in interesting fashion at the Old Water-Colour Society's. She happened to be there during the Exhibition of 1877 at a time when the room was almost empty. Mr. Ruskin had been looking at her drawing of Carlyle, and introducing himself, asked her why she had painted Carlyle like a lamb, when he ought to be painted like a lion, as he was, and whether she would paint the sage as such for him?. To this she had to reply that she could only paint him as she saw him, which was certainly not in leonine garb. One afternoon soon afterwards, Mr. Allingham chanced to meet Ruskin at Carlyle's, and brought him round to see her work. She was

[1] See *Letters of Dante Gabriel Rossetti to William Allingham.* (London: Fisher Unwin, 1897.)

at the time engaged on the drawing of "The Clothes-Line" (Plate 11), and he objected to the scarlet of the handkerchief, and also to the woman, who he said ought to have been a rough work-woman, an opinion which Mrs. Allingham did not share with him at the time, but which she has since felt to be a correct one.   He also saw another drawing with a grey sky, and asked her why she did not make her skies blue.   To her reply that she thought there was often great beauty in grey skies, he growled, "The devil sends grey skies."

Browning, an old friend of her husband's, Mrs. Allingham sometimes had the privilege of seeing during her residence in London.   One occasion was typical of the man.   He had been asked to come and see her work, which was at the time arranged at one end of a room at Trafalgar Square, Chelsea, before sending in to the Exhibition.   The drawings were naturally small ones, and Browning appeared to be altogether oblivious to their exist-ence.   Turning round, with his back to them, he at once commenced a story of some one who came to see an artist's work, and the artist was very huffed because his visitor never took the slightest notice of his pictures, but talked to him of other subjects all the time. This, Browning considered, was no sufficient ground for his huffiness. His obliviousness to Mrs. Allingham's drawings may have been due to his having been accustomed to the pictures of his son, which were of large size, and in comparison with which Mrs. Allingham's would be quite invisible. Against this theory, however, I may mention that on one occasion I happened to have the good fortune to be present in his son's studio when Tennyson was announced. Browning at once advanced to the door to meet him, bent low, and addressed him as " Magister Meus," and although the Laureate had come to see the paintings, and stayed some time, neither of the two poets, so long as I was present, noticed them in any way.

Whilst Mrs. Allingham was painting Carlyle, Browning came to see him, and they held a most interesting and delightful conversation on the subject of the great French writers. The alteration in Browning's demeanour from his usual bluff and breezy manner to a quiet, deferential tone during the conversation was very notable.

Of her intimacy with Tennyson I may speak later when we come to the drawings which illustrate his two houses in Sussex and the Isle of Wight.

The year of her marriage was also a landmark
in Mrs. Allingham's career, through the Royal
Academy accepting and hanging two water-colours,
one entitled "The Milkmaid," the other, "Wait
for Me," the subject of the latter being a young
lady entering a cottage whilst a dog watched her
outside the gate.   It would have been interesting
to have been able to insert a reproduction of either
of these in this volume, for they would probably
have shown that her fear as to her inability to
master colour was entirely without basis, but I
have not been able to trace them.   The drawings
were not only well hung, but were sold during the
Exhibition.

It was, however, by another drawing that Mrs.
Allingham won her name.

In the year 1875 she was commissioned by Mr.
George Bell to make a water-colour from one of
the black-and-white drawings which she had done
some years before for Mrs. Ewing's *A Flat Iron
for a Farthing*.   We shall have occasion to de-
scribe at length, later on, this delightful little
picture that is reproduced in Plate 8.   It is only
necessary for our purpose here to state that it was
seen early in 1875 by that prince of landscape
water-colourists, Mr. Alfred Hunt.

He was an old friend of Mr. Allingham's, and being told that his wife was thinking of trying for election at the Royal Society of Painters in Water Colours, kindly offered to go through her portfolios. From these he made a selection, and promised to propose her at an election which was about to take place. The result fully proved the soundness of his choice, for the candidate not only secured the rare distinction of being elected on the first time of asking, but the still rarer one of securing her place in that body, so notable for its diversity of opinion when candidates are in question, with hardly a dissentient vote.

Ladies were not admitted to the rank of full members of the Society until the year 1890, when she was, to her great pleasure and astonishment, elected a full member. She deserved it; for much of the charm of these exhibitions had been due to the presence of the work which she has contributed to every Exhibition held since her election save two, one of these rare absences being due to her having mistaken the date for sending in.

This election, and the fact that after her marriage she could afford to do without the monetary aid derived from black-and-white work, decided her to embark upon water-colours; although

in these she still confined her work to figure subjects,
more than one of which continued to be founded
on her previous work in monochrome.

The last book in which her name as an illustrator appeared was, appropriately enough, *Rhymes
for the Young Folk*, by her husband, published
in *Cassell's* in 1885, to which she contributed
most of the illustrations. She relinquished black-
and-white work without any regret, for although
she was much indebted to it, it never held her
sympathies, and she always longed to express
herself in colour, the medium in which she in-
stinctively felt she had ultimately the best chance
of success.

Although we are only separated from the
Chelsea of Mrs. Allingham's days by little more
than a quarter of a century, its artistic associations were then of a very different order to those
that are in evidence nowadays. The era of vast
studios in which duchesses and millionaires find
adequate surroundings for their portraits was not
yet. Whistler was close to old Chelsea Church,
a few doors only from where he recently died. Tite
Street, with which his name will always be connected, was not yet built. He was still engaged
on those remarkable, but at that time insuffi-

ciently appreciated, canvases of scenes which have now passed away, such as " Fireworks at Cremorne," and " Nocturnes " dimly disclosing old Battersea Bridge.   Seymour Haden was etching the picturesque façade of the Walk, with his brother-in-law's house as a principal object in it, and without the respectable embankment which now makes it more reputable from a hygienic, but less admirable from an artistic point of view. Rossetti was practically the only other artist of note in the quarter.   But with one exception Mrs. Allingham's work was not reminiscent of the place.   That exception, however, disclosed to her a field in which she foresaw much delight and abundant possibilities.   In the old Pensioners' Garden at Chelsea Hospital were to be found tenderly - cared - for borders of humble flowers. The garden itself was a haven of repose for the old warriors, and a show-place for their visitors. Mrs. Allingham, like another artist, Hubert Herkomer, about the same time, was touched by the pathos of the surroundings, and, chiefly on the urgency of her husband, she ventured on a drawing of more importance than any hitherto attempted. The subject, which we shall speak of again later, was finished in 1877, and was the first large drawing exhibited by her at the Society of Painters in Water Colours.

Painters—good, bad, and indifferent—of the garden are nowadays such a numerous body that one is apt to forget that the time is quite recent when to paint one with its flowers was a new departure. It is nevertheless the fact, and in taking it up, especially those that are associated with the humbler type of cottages, Mrs. Allingham was practically the originator of a new subject. To the pensioners' patches at Chelsea we are indebted for the sweet portraits of humble flowersteads which are now cherished by so many a fortunate possessor, and charm every beholder. Thus Chelsea aroused a desire to attack gardens possessing greater possibilities than a town-stunted patch, a desire that was not, however, gratified until two years later when, during a visit in the spring of 1879 to Shere, the first of many cottages and flowers was painted from nature.

In 1881, after the death of Carlyle, Chelsea had attractions for neither husband nor wife, and with a young family growing up and calling for larger and healthier quarters, the house in Trafalgar Square was given up for one at Witley in Surrey, a hamlet close to Haslemere, which she had visited the year before, and in the midst of a country which Birket Foster had already done much to popularise, having resided at a beautiful house there for many years.

———

THE water-colours of this first period, namely from 1875 to 1880, that are reproduced here, are the following :—

8. THE YOUNG CUSTOMERS

From the Water-colour in the possession of Miss Bell.

Painted 1875.

The drawing by which, as we have said, Mrs. Allingham made her name, obtained election at the Society of Painters in Water Colours, was represented at her first appearance there in 1875, and also at the Paris Exposition in 1878, and through which she obtained the recognition of Ruskin, who thus wrote concerning it in the *Notes* which he was at that time in the habit of compiling each year on the Summer Exhibitions,

It happens curiously that the only drawing of which the
memory remains with me as a possession out of the Old Water-
Colour Exhibition of this year—Mrs. Allingham's "Young
Customers"—should not only be by an accomplished designer
of woodcuts, but itself the illustration of a popular story.
The drawing, with whatever temporary purpose executed, is
for ever lovely—a thing which I believe Gainsborough would
have given one of his own paintings for, old fashioned as red-
tipped daisies are, and more precious than rubies.

Later on, in 1883, in his lectures at Oxford on
Mrs. Allingham he again referred to it as "The
drawing which some years ago riveted, and ever
since has retained the public admiration—the two
deliberate housewives in their village toyshop, bent
on domestic utilities and economies, and proud in
the acquisition of two flat irons for a farthing—has
become, and rightly, a classic picture, which will
have its place among the memorable things in the
Art of our time, when many of its loudly-trumpeted
magnificences are remembered no more."

The black-and-white drawing on which it was
founded, a somewhat thin and immature performance, was one of twelve illustrations made by
Mrs. Allingham for Mrs. Ewing's *A Flat Iron for
a Farthing*,[1] where it appears as illustrating the

---

[1] *A Flat Iron for a Farthing, or some Passages in the Life of an Only
Son*, by Juliana Horatia Ewing.   (George Bell and Sons.)

following episode. It will be seen that Mrs. Allingham's version of the story differs in many points from that of the authoress, which is thus told by Reginald, the only son :—

As I looked, there came down the hill a fine, large, sleek donkey, led by an old man-servant, and having on its back what is called a Spanish saddle, in which two little girls sat side by side, the whole party jogging quietly along at a foot's pace in the sunshine. I was so overwhelmed and impressed by the loveliness of these two children, and by their quaint, queenly little ways, that time has not dimmed one line in the picture that they then made upon my mind. I can see them now as clearly as I saw them then, as I stood at the tinsmith's door in the High Street of Oakford—let me see, how many years ago?

The child who looked the older, but was, as I afterwards discovered, the younger of the two, was also the less pretty. And yet she had a sweet little face, hair like spun gold, and blue-grey eyes with dark lashes. She wore a grey frock of some warm material, below which peeped her indoors dress of blue. The outer coat had a quaint cape like a coachman's, which was relieved by a broad white crimped frill round her throat. Her legs were cased in knitted gaiters of white wool, and her hands in the most comical miniatures of gloves. On her fairy head she wore a large bonnet of grey beaver, with a frill inside. But it was her sister who shone on my young eyes like a fairy vision. She looked too delicate, too brilliant, too utterly lovely, for anywhere but fairyland.

She ought to have been kept in tissue-paper, like the loveliest of wax dolls. Her hair was the true flaxen, the very fairest of the fair. The purity and vividness of the tints of red and white in her face I have never seen equalled. Her eyes were of speedwell blue, and looked as if they were meant to be always more or less brimming with tears. To say the truth, her face had not half the character which gave force to that of the other little damsel, but a certain helplessness about it gave it a peculiar charm. She was dressed exactly like the other, with one exception—her bonnet was of white beaver, and she became it like a queen.

At the tinsmith's shop they stopped, and the old man-servant, after unbuckling a strap which seemed to support them in their saddle, lifted each little miss in turn to the ground. Once on the pavement the little lady of the grey beaver shook herself out, and proceeded to straighten the disarranged overcoat of her companion, and then, taking her by the hand, the two clambered up the step into the shop. The tinsmith's shop boasted of two seats, and on to one of these she of the grey beaver with some difficulty climbed. The eyes of the other were fast filling with tears, when from her lofty perch the sister caught sight of the man-servant, who stood in the doorway, and she beckoned him with a wave of her tiny finger.

" Lift her up, if you please," she said on his approach. And the other child was placed on the other chair.

The shopman appeared to know them, and though he smiled, he said very respectfully, " What articles can I show you this morning, ladies ? "

The fairy-like creature in the white beaver, who had been fumbling in her miniature glove, now timidly laid a farthing on the counter, and then turning her back for very shyness on the shopman, raised one small shoulder, and inclining her head towards it, gave an appealing glance at her sister out of the pale-blue eyes. That little lady, thus appealed to, firmly placed another farthing on the board, and said in the tiniest but most decided of voices,

"Two FLAT IRONS, IF YOU PLEASE."

Hereupon the shopman produced a drawer from below the counter, and set it before them. What it contained I was not tall enough to see, but out of it he took several flat irons of triangular shape, and apparently made of pewter, or some alloy of tin. These the grey beaver examined and tried upon a corner of her cape, with inimitable gravity and importance. At last she selected two, and keeping one for herself, gave the other to her sister.

"Is it a nice one?" the little white-beavered lady inquired.

"Very nice."

"Kite as nice as yours?" she persisted.

"Just the same," said the other firmly. And having glanced at the counter to see that the farthings were both duly deposited, she rolled abruptly over on her seat, and scrambled off backwards, a manœuvre which the other child accomplished with more difficulty. The coats and capes were then put tidy as before, and the two went out of the shop together, hand in hand.

Then the old man-servant lifted them into the Spanish

saddle, and buckled the strap, and away they went up the steep street, and over the brow of the hill, where trees and palings began to show, the beaver bonnets nodding together in consultation over the flat irons.

The commission to paint this water-colour being unfettered in every way, the artist felt herself at liberty to create a colour scheme of her own—hence the changes in the dresses, etc. ; also to put an old woman (after a Devonshire cottager) in place of the shopman, and to make the shop a toyshop instead of a tinsmith's.   The little girl ironing was painted from a study of a Mr. Hennessy's eldest little daughter ; the fair little maiden from Mr. Briton Riviere's eldest daughter.

9. THE SAND-MARTINS' HAUNT

From the Water-colour in the possession of Miss James.

Painted 1876.

I passed an inland cliff precipitate ;
   From tiny caves peeped many a soot-black poll.
In each a mother-martin sat elate,
   And of the news delivered her small soul :
" Gossip, how wags the world ?"   " Well, gossip, well."

Interesting not only as the earliest example here of Mrs. Allingham's landscape work, having been

painted at Limpsfield, Surrey, in May 1876, and
as such full of promise of better things to come,
but as an instance of a preference for a complex
and very difficult effect, which the artist, on obtaining greater experience, very wisely abandoned.
There is little doubt that she was tempted by the
glorious wealth of colouring which a low sun threw
upon the warm quarry side, the pine wood, and
the huge cumuli which banked them up—a magnificent but a fleeting effect, which could only
be placed on record from very rapid notes. The
result could be successful only in the hands of a
practised adept, and it is not surprising, therefore,
that in those of an artist just embarking on her
career it was not entirely so. The difficulties of
the task may have afforded her a useful lesson,
for we have seen no further attempts on her part
at their repetition.

If the landscape foretells little concerning the
future of the artist, the figures standing on the brink
of the quarry, the elder with her arm placed lovingly
and protectingly round the neck of the younger,
whilst they watch the martins rejoicing in the warm
summer evening, are eminently suggestive of the
success which Mrs. Allingham was to achieve in
the addition of figures to landscape composition.

10. THE OLD MEN'S GARDENS, CHELSEA HOSPITAL

From the Water-colour in the possession of Mr. Charles Churchill.

Painted 1876.

Contemporary criticism is not, as a rule, palatable to an artist, for amongst the varied views which the art critics bring to their task there are always to be found some that are not seen from the same standpoint as his.   Besides, for some occult reason, the balance always trends in the direction of fault-finding rather than praise, probably because it is so much the easier, for work always has and will have imperfections that are not difficult to distinguish.   But in the case of the water-colour before us the critics' chorus must have been very exhilarating to the young artist, especially as, at the time of its exhibition at the Royal Water-Colour Society, in the spring of 1877, she was by no means in good health.   The *Spectator*, for instance, wrote that artists would have to look to their laurels when ladies began to paint in a manner little inferior to Walker.   The *Athenæum* gave it the exceptional length of a column, considering it "one of the few pictures by which

the exhibition in question would be remembered."
Tom Taylor in the *Times* wrote as follows :—

Of all the newly associated figure painters there is none
whose work has more of the rare quality that inspires interest
than Mrs. Allingham.   She has only two drawings here, a
pretty little child's head and a large and exquisitely finished
composition, "The Old Men's Gardens, Chelsea Hospital,"
where some hundred and forty little garden plots are parcelled
out among as many of the old pensioners, each of whom is
free to follow his own fancies in his gardening.

In the hush of a calm summer evening, two graceful girls
in white dresses accept a nosegay from one of the veterans,
a Guardsman of the *vieille cour*, by his look and bearing.
All around are plots of sweet, bright flowers all aglow with
variegated petals.   Here and there under the shade of the
old trees sit restful groups of the old veterans, with children
about them ; one little fellow reverentially lifts and examines
one of the medals on a war-worn breast.   Behind, the
thickly-clothed fronds of a drooping ash spread to the
declining sun, and the level roofs of the old Hospital rise
ruddy against the warm and cloudless sky.   No praise can
be too high for the exquisiteness with which the flowers are
drawn, coloured, and combined, or for the skill with which
they are blended into an artistic whole with the suggestive
and graceful group in the foreground.   The drawing deserves
to take its place as a pendant of Walker's "Haven of Rest."

It is curious that all the critics seem to have

misinterpreted the main meaning of the artist's
motive, namely, that whilst the Pensioners naturally, in the first place, wish to sell their posies,
they are always ready to give them to those who
cannot afford to buy.   The well-to-do ladies are
purchasing the flowers, the little group of mother,
boy, and baby, on the right, who can ill afford to
buy, are having a posy graciously offered to them.
The drawing represented Mrs. Allingham at the
Jubilee Exhibition in Manchester, 1887, and the
Loan Water-Colour Exhibition at the Guildhall,
London, in 1896.   It is of the large size, for this
artist's work, of 25 inches by 15 inches.

11. THE CLOTHES-LINE

From the Water-colour in the possession of Miss James.

Painted 1879.

How considerable and rapid an advance now
took place in Mrs. Allingham's powers may be seen
from the two drawings which are dated two years
later, namely, in 1879. In figure draftsmanship there
is no comparison between the timid and haltingly
painted children of "The Sand-Martins' Haunt"
and the seated baby in "The Clothes-Line." In

the first the capacity to draw was no doubt present,
but the power to express it through the medium of
water-colour was as yet unacquired.   But after two
years' study, knowledge is present in its fulness, and
from now onwards the only changes in Mrs. Allingham's work are a greater precision, breadth, facility
of handling, and harmony of colour.   The figure of
the woman still smacks somewhat too much of the
studio, and she is a lady-like model,[1] certainly not
the type one would expect to see hanging out the
washing of such a clearly limited and humble
wardrobe as in this case.   The figure again detaches
itself too much from the rest of the picture, and
Mrs. Allingham, we are sure, would now never
introduce such a jarring note as the scarlet
and primrose handkerchief, to which Mr. Ruskin
objected at the time it was painted.   The blanket,
clothes-line, clothes-basket, and other accessories
are painted with a minuteness which was an admir-

---

[1] The model was a Mrs. Stewart, who, with her husband, sat to Mrs.
Allingham for years.   They were well known in art circles, and had
charge of the Hogarth Club, Fitzroy Square, when Mrs. Allingham,
before her marriage, lived in Southampton Row close by.   She introduced the models to Mr. du Maurier, who immediately engaged them,
and continued to use them for many years.   " Ponsonby de Tompkins "
was Stewart, run to seed, and " Mrs. Ponsonby de Tompkins " a very
good portrait of Mrs. Stewart.

able prelude to the breadth that was to follow ; but are singularly constrained in comparison with the yellow gorse bushes, most difficult of any shrubs to limn, but which here are noteworthy for unusual easiness of touch.   Even with these qualifications the picture is a delightful one, replete with grace and beauty, and complete in its portrayal of the little incident of the baby, a less robust little body than Mrs. Allingham would now paint, capturing as many of the clothes-pegs that her mother needs as her small fingers and arms can embrace.

12. THE CONVALESCENT

From the Water-colour in the possession of Mr. R. S. Budgett.

Painted 1879.

This, like "The Young Customers," was founded on previous work, namely, a black-and-white drawing made for the *Graphic*, as an illustration to Mrs. Oliphant's *Innocent*.   But in the story the patient dies from an over-dose administered in mistake by Innocent, who is nursing her.   Some years afterwards the poisoning comes to light, and Innocent is tried and acquitted.   Mrs. Allingham would never have voluntarily repeated such a subject as this,

and her temperament is shown in her having
utilised the material for one in which refreshing
sleep promises a speedy recovery.

13. THE GOAT CARRIAGE

From the Water-colour in the possession of Sir F. Wigan.

Painted 1880.

Painted at Broadstairs, and containing portraits
of Mrs. Allingham's children.   Noticeable as being
one of a few drawings where the artist has introduced animals of any size into her compositions,
but showing that, had she minded, she might have
animated her landscapes with them with as con-
spicuous success as she has with her human figures.
Perhaps an incident which happened whilst this
picture was being painted deterred her.   Billy
being tied up so as to keep him in somewhat the
same position, managed to gnaw through his rope,
and, irate at his detention, he made for the lady to
whom he thought his captivity was due, and nearly
upset her, paintbox, and picture.   The exhibition
of this and kindred portraits of her children under
such titles as "The Young Artist" and "The
Donkey Ride," led to strangers wishing for por-

traits of their offspring under similar winsome conditions. But Mrs. Allingham never cared for the restraint imposed by portrait painting, and the few that she did in this manner were undertaken more from friendship than from pleasure.

14. THE CLOTHES-BASKET

From the Water-colour the property of Mr. C. P. Johnson.

Painted 1880.

It is very seldom that Mrs. Allingham has treated her public to drawings with low horizons or sunsets, perhaps for the reason that little of her life has been spent away in the flatter counties, where the latter are so noticeable and full of charm and beauty. This water-colour, the first large landscape that the artist exhibited, was painted from studies made in the Isle of Thanet, whilst staying at Broadstairs.

15. IN THE HAYLOFT

From the Water-colour the property of Miss Bell.

Painted 1880.

This is practically the last of the water-colours

which were the outcome of earlier pictures executed in black and white for the illustration of books.

The story is from *Deborah's Drawer*, by Eleanor Grace O'Reilly, for which, as Helen Paterson, our artist had made nine drawings in 1870, at a time when she was so inexperienced in drawing on the wood that in more than one instance her monogram appears turned the wrong way. Mr. Bell, the publisher of the book, subsequently commissioned her to make a companion water-colour to "The Young Customers," and suggested one of the illustrations called "Ralph's Girls" as the basis for a subject.

The little black-robed girls were twins, whose mother had recently died, and who had been placed under the care of a grandmother, who forgot their youth and spirits. They were imaginative children, and indulged in delightfully original games. One (that of personating a sportsman named Jenkins and a dog called Tubbs, who together went part-ridge-shooting through a big field of cabbages laden with dew) they had just been taking part in. Tired out with it, they decided to be themselves again, and to mount to the hayloft and play another favourite game, that of "remembering." This meant taking them back over their short lives, which ended up with their most recent remembrance, their mother's death. Whilst talking over this they are summoned from their retreat, and have to appear with their black dresses soaked with the dew from the cabbages, and with hay adhering everywhere to their deep crape trimmings. Hence much penance !

16. THE RABBIT HUTCH

From the Drawing the property of Mr. C. P. Johnson.

Painted 1880.

Painted in London, but from sketches made near Broadstairs, the house seen over the wall being one of those that are to be found along the east coast, which bear a decided evidence of Dutch influence in their architecture. Here again we have evidence that Mrs. Allingham might, had she been so minded, have succeeded with animals as well as she has with human figures and landscape. A little play is being enacted ; the dog, evidently a rival of the inhabitants of the hutch, has to be kept at a distance while their feeding is going on, lest his jealousy might find an outlet in an onslaught upon them.

17. THE DONKEY RIDE

From the Water-colour in the possession of
Sir James Kitson, Bart., M.P.

Painted 1880.

This drawing was executed just at the turning
of the ways, when London was to be exchanged for
country life, and studio for out-of-door painting.
What an increased power came about through the
change will be seen by a comparison between this
"Donkey Ride" and the "Children's Tea" (Plate 23).
Only two years separate them in date ; but whilst
in the one we have timidity and hesitancy, in the
other the end is practically assured.   In "The
Donkey Ride" we have evidences of experiments,
especially in the direction of finicking stippling (all
over the sea and sky) and of the use of body-colour
(in the baby's bonnet and the flowers), which were
abandoned later on, to the artist's exceeding great
benefit.   What we expect to find, and do find, is
the pure sentiment, and the dainty freshness, which
is never absent from the earliest efforts onwards.

The scene is the cliffs near Broadstairs, Mrs.
Allingham's two eldest children occupying the
panniers.

CHAPTER IV

THE ARTIST'S SURREY HOME

THERE are few fairer counties in England than Surrey, and of Surrey the fairest portion is admittedly the extreme south-western edge which skirts Sussex to the south and Hampshire to the west. Travellers from London to Portsmouth by the London and South-Western Railway on leaving Guildford pass through the middle of the right angle which this corner makes, and cut the corner two miles beyond Haslemere almost exactly at the point where the three counties meet. As the steep rise of nearly 300 feet which has to be surmounted in the six miles which divide Witley from Haslemere is being negotiated by the train, the most unobservant passenger must be struck by the singularly beautiful wooded character of the country on either side, and by the far-extended

view which is unfolded as the eye looks southward over the Weald of Sussex.

It was to Sandhills, near Witley, that Mrs.
Allingham came to live in 1881 with her growing
family, and it was in this corner of Surrey that she
found ample material for almost all her work during
the next few years; and it is there that she has
returned at intervals for the majority of those
cottage subjects which the public has called for,
ever since her first portrayal of them shortly after
her commencement of landscape painting in these
parts.

Witley consists of groups of irregularly-dotted-
about houses, which hardly constitute a village, and
would perhaps be better designated by the proper
name—Witley Street.   A few years ago every one
of the houses counted their ages by centuries, and
were fitting companions of the ancient oaks and
elms that shaded them.   Some few are left, but
the majority are gone, many so long before the
term of their natural existence had run that it was
a troublesome piece of work to destroy them.
There is also an old "Domesday Book" Church.
Drawings of almost all of the cottages, from the
hand of Mrs. Allingham, are in existence somewhere
or other, but she never seems to have painted this

or other churches, having apparently little liking
for them, as had Birket Foster. In the present
case the omission to do so arose from the fact that
in painting it she would have formed one of the
occupants of half-a-dozen outspread white umbrellas, all taking a stiffly-composed subject from
the same point of view.

Sandhills, where our artist lived, is on the
Haslemere side of Witley, on a sloping common of
heather and gorse, topped with fir trees. From
thence the view, looking southwards, extends far
and wide over the Weald of Surrey and Sussex,
Hindhead, a mountain-like hill rising behind, and
Blackdown, a spur stretching out on to the Sussex
Valley to the right.   In the distance are to be seen
the rising grounds near Midhurst and Petworth,
Chanctonbury Ring with its tuft of trees, called
locally "The Squire's Hunting Cap," and on a
clear day the downs as far as Brighton and Lewes.

It is indeed a healthy and bracing spot, and one
calculated to induce a painter to energetic work,
and a delight in doing it. Subjects lay close at
hand, the Sandhills garden furnishing many a one.
"Master Hardy's," a charming cottage tenanted by
a charming old man, was within a stone's throw,
and received attention inside and out. Of the

Hindhead Road, which passes south-west, a single
Exhibition, that of 1886, contained six subjects, all
of them wayside cottages, but no one of which,
when the Exhibition opened, was as depicted,
having in that short time been "done up" by local
builders at the bidding of Philistine owners.

The neighbourhood round is, or perhaps we
should say was, also prolific in subjects—Haslemere, four miles south-west, with its pleasant wide
old streets, and with fields tilted up at the end of
it, furnished its Fish-Shop, and other thoroughly
English village scenes.

Some two miles south of Haslemere was Aldworth, Lord Tennyson's house, a mile over the
Sussex border, although always spoken of as his
"Surrey" residence. To Mrs. Allingham's work
there we shall have occasion to refer later on.

The varied summits of Hindhead (painted a
century earlier by Turner and Rowlandson, and at
that time adorned with a gibbet for the benefit
of the highwaymen who infested the Portsmouth
Road, which passes over it), in one place bare
moor, in another crested with fir trees, lay some
distance northward of Haslemere; but our artist
did not often depict them, although they presented
themselves under many a charming aspect, and

18. A WITLEY LANE

19. HINDHEAD FROM WITLEY COMMON

20. IN WITLEY VILLAGE

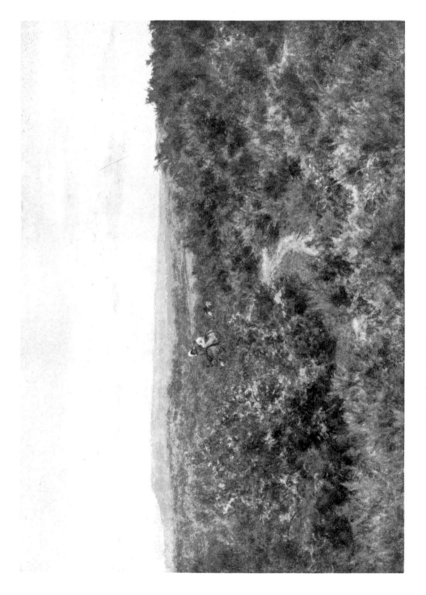

21. BLACKDOWN FROM WITLEY COMMON

22. THE FISH-SHOP, HASLEMERE

23. THE CHILDREN'S TEA

24. THE STILE

25. "PAT-A-CAKE"

26. LESSONS

27. BUBBLES

28. ON THE SANDS—SANDOWN, ISLE OF WIGHT

29. DRYING CLOTHES

30. HER MAJESTY'S POST OFFICE

31. THE CHILDREN'S MAYPOLE

32. SPRING ON THE KENTISH DOWNS

33. TIG BRIDGE

never more glorious than at sunset in their robes
of violet and gold.   A thoroughly characteristic
view of them is however given in the Lord Chief
Justice's drawing (Plate 19).

To the southward of Sandhills stretches, as we
have said, the Weald.   To this district Mrs.
Allingham made frequent excursions, not only for
cottages, which she found at Hambledon, Chiddingfold, and Wisborough, but for spring and autumn
subjects in the oak woods and copses which to this
day probably bear much the same aspect as did the
ancient Forest of Anderida (whose site they occupy)
in the time of the Heptarchy.

Oak is the tree of the wealden clay on the lower
levels, but elms grow to a grand size on the higher
ground, where ashes are also numerous.   Spanish
chestnuts "encamp in state" on certain slopes, and
many of the hills are "fringed and pillared" with
pines.   The interminable hazel copses are inter-
spersed with long labyrinthine paths, the intricacies
of which are only known to the countryside folk.
Not so long ago the cutting down at intervals of
the young wood for the purposes of hop poles,
hurdles, and kindling, brought in a handsome
revenue to the owners; but of late years wire has
taken the place of wood for the two first of these

objects, and the labourers prefer dear coal to wood, even at a gift, for it does not entail cutting up. As railway rates to bring it to the metropolis are prohibitive, it is hard to say what the consequences will be in a few years, but the probabilities actually point to a return to the primitive conditions which existed in the Saxon times to which we have referred.

In the spring the country round is decked with primroses, bluebells, and cowslips in the woods, hedgerows, and fields, being fortunately outside the range of the marauders from London; and it is indeed pleasurable to ramble from copse to field, and back again. But in autumn and winter the deep clay soil makes it heavy travelling in the deep-cut roads and lanes, cumbered with the redolent decay of the leafage from the trees.

The cottars were, when the majority of these drawings were made, rural and old-fashioned, and many had lived hereabouts through numerous generations. A quiet, taciturn folk, contented with moderate comforts, on good terms with their wealthier neighbours, not often feeling the pinch of poverty.

Maybe all are not so good-looking as Mrs. Allingham has depicted them, but they vary much,

some being flaxen Saxons, others as dark com-
plexioned as gipsies.

As will be seen, they have a taste and enjoyment for colour, if not for change, in the gardens
with which their cottages are fairly well supplied.
These are bright at one or other season of the year
with snowdrop, crocus, and daffodil, lilac, sweet·
william, and pink, sunflower, Michaelmas daisy
and chrysanthemum.

THE following drawings have been selected as
illustrating the neighbourhood of Mrs. Allingham's
home at Sandhills :—

18. A WITLEY LANE

From the Water-colour in the possession of Mr. H. W Birks.

Painted 1887.

IT is very seldom that we encounter a drawing
of Mrs. Allingham that deals with Nature in
winter's garb.   In this respect she differs from
Birket Foster, who rightly considered that trees

were oftentimes as beautiful in their nude as in
their clothed array.   Especially did he delight in
the towering framework of the elm, which he regarded as the most typical of English trees.

Nor is it often that we see Mrs. Allingham
afield so early in the spring as in this lane scene,
where the elms are clothed only in their "ruddy
hearted blossom flakes."[1]   Perhaps this absence is
due to prudential reasons, to avoid the rheumatism
which appears to be the only ailment which the
landscapist runs against in his healthy outdoor
profession.

Those who have seen the woods of Surrey and
Sussex at this time of year know what a lovely
colour they assume in the budding stage, a colour
that makes the view over the Weald from such
a vantage-ground as Blackdown a sea of ravishing
violet hues, almost equalling that of the oak forests
as seen in February from the Terrace at Pau, which
stretch away to the snow-clad range of the Pyre-
nees—perhaps the most delicately perfect view in
Europe.   But the day selected for this sketch was
evidently a warm one for the time of year, or we

[1] Lord Tennyson quoted this line to Mrs. Allingham one day when,
walking with him, they passed ground covered with the fallen flowers
of the lime trees.

should not see that unusual occurrence, an open bedroom window in a labourer's cottage.

The flowering whin is no index to the season, for we know the old adage—

When the whin's in bloom, my love's in tune.

But the catkins on the hazel, and the primroses on the banks, must place it round that elastic date, Eastertide.

These wayside primroses remind one of a strongly expressed opinion of Mrs. Allingham's, that wayside flowers should never be gathered, but left for the enjoyment of the passers-by—a liberal one, which was first instilled into her by her husband, who wrote verses upon it, from which I cull the following lines :—

> Pluck not the wayside flower,
> It is the traveller's dower;
> A thousand passers-by
> Its beauties may espy.
>
> .   .
>
> The primrose on the slope
> A spot of sunshine dwells,
> And cheerful message tells.
>
> .   .   '
>
> Then spare the wayside flower
> It is the traveller's dower.

19. HINDHEAD FROM WITLEY COMMON

*From the Water-colour in the possession of the Lord Chief Justice
of England.*

Painted 1888.

When this drawing appeared in the Exhibition
of 1889 there were some who called in question
the truthfulness of the colour of distant Hindhead,
affirming that it was too blue.   But when the air
comes up in August from the southward, laden
with a salty moisture, and the shadows are cast by
hurrying clouds over the distance, it is altogether
and exactly of the hue set down here.   Had the
effect been incorrect it would hardly have been
acquired by so critical a collector as Lord Alverstone, nor would it have been hung in his Surrey
home, where it invites daily comparison with Nature
under similar aspects.   The drawing was painted on
the spot, from just behind the artist's house, and
is one of the few instances where she has added to
the charm of her work by a sky of some intricacy.
In her cottage and other drawings, where buildings
or other landscape objects are of primary importance, she has felt that the simpler the treatment of
the sky the better, and with good reason.   Here,

where a large expanse calls for interesting forms to cover it, she has shown her complete ability to introduce them.

Mrs. Allingham's house at Sandhills was below the foreground slope, to the right of the cottages whose roofs rise from the ling. The highest point of Hindhead seen here is Hurt Hill, some nine hundred feet above sea-level, a name which Mr. Allingham always held to be a corruption of Whort Hill, from the whortleberries with which its slopes are covered, and which in these, as in other parts are called " wurts."

20. IN WITLEY VILLAGE

From the Water-colour in the possession of Mr. Charles Churchill.

Painted 1884.

This drawing was in The Fine Art Society's Exhibition in 1886, the catalogue stating that the cottage had disappeared in the spring of 1885. It was pulled down by its owner to be replaced by buildings whose monotonous symmetry, to his eye no doubt, appeared in better taste. The cottage was still far from the natural term of its existence, as evidenced by the troublesome piece of work it was to dislocate the sound, firm old oaken beams of which its framework was built up. Mr. Birket Foster, who equally with Mrs. Allingham mourned its disappearance, regretted that he could not rebuild it in his own grounds.

The blackening elms, and the ripe bracken carried home by the cottar, show that the time when this picturesque dwelling was painted was late summer, probably that of 1884. Mrs. Allingham was clearly then not of Ruskin's opinion concerning the wrongness of painting trees in full leaf, for she found the blue-black of the trees a harmonious background to her red and russet roof.

The work throughout shows a loving fidelity to Nature, as if the artist had felt that she was looking upon the likeness of an old friend for the last time, and wished to perpetuate every lineament and feature.

21. BLACKDOWN FROM WITLEY COMMON

From the Water-colour in the possession of Lord Davey.

Painted 1886.

This view is taken from the same bridle-path as is seen in Lord Alverstone's "Hindhead," but at a lower elevation, and looking some points more to the south ; also at a later time of year, probably in early October, to judge by the browning hazels. The bracken-covered elevation in the distance is Grays Wood Common, which lies to the south of the railway, and the spur of blue hill seen in the distance is Blackdown.   Aldworth, Lord Tennyson's seat, lies just this side of where the hill falls away.   The drawing is one of three only in the whole collection where Mrs. Allingham has introduced a draught animal.

22. THE FISH-SHOP, HASLEMERE

From the Water-colour in the possession of Mr. A. E. Cumberbatch.

Painted 1887.

One can well understand the local builder in his daily round past this picturesque little tenement casting longing eyes upon its uneven roof, its diamond-paned lattices, its projecting shop front, and its spoutless eaves, which allowed the damp to rise up from the foundations and the green lichen to grow upon its walls, and that he rested not until he had set hands upon it, and taken one more old-world feature from the main thoroughfare

at Haslemere.   Such was actually the case here,
for the shop has long ago disappeared, but it was
not until, much to its owner's regret, interference
was necessary.   Were it not that it indeed was the
fish-shop of Haslemere, it might well have served
for the toyshop in which the scene of "The Young
Customers" was laid.   In the days when this was
painted the accommodation provided was probably
sufficient for the intermittent supply of an inland
village, for Haslemere was not, until the last few
years, a country resort for those who seek fine air
and beautiful scenery, and can afford to pay a high
price for it.

CHAPTER V

IT will be readily understood that such a beneficial change in her life surroundings as that from Trafalgar Square, Chelsea, to Sandhills, Witley, was not without its effect upon Mrs. Allingham's Art. Hitherto her work had, by the exigencies of fortune, lain almost wholly and entirely in the direction of the figure. It was studio work, done for the most part under pressure of time, the selection of subject being none of hers, and therefore oftentimes altogether unsympathetic. Finding herself now in the presence of Nature of a kind that appealed to her, and which she could appreciate untrammelled by any conditions, it is not surprising that—unwittingly, no doubt, at first—the preference was given to that side of Art which presented itself under so much more favourable conditions.

The delight of painting *en plein air* had first

been tasted at Shere in the spring and summer of 1878, where she was passionately happy in watching the changes and developments of the seasons, being in the fields, lanes, and copses all day and every day.[1] Almost as full a feast had followed at Haslemere in 1880. When these were succeeded by a permanent residence in front of Nature, studio work became more and more trying and unsatisfactory.

To most people of an artistic temperament the abandonment of the figure for landscape would never have been the subject of a moment's consideration, for it would have appeared to them the desertion of a higher for a lower grade of Art. But from the time of her arrival in the country there seems to have never been any doubt in Mrs. Allingham's mind as to the direction which her Art should take. The pleasure to which we have referred of sitting down in the open air before Nature, whose aspects and moods she could select at her own will, and at her own time, was infinitely preferable to the toil and trouble of either illustrating the ideas of others, or building up scenes, often-

---

[1] I have been reminded by the artist that my first introduction to her was at Trafalgar Square, Chelsea, whither I went to see the products of this Shere visit, and that I came away with some of them in my possession.

times improbable ones, of her own creation. From this time onwards, then, we find her drifting away from the figure, but not altogether, or at once, for as her family grew up, scenes in her house life passed across her view which she enjoyed to place on record, and for which the world thanks her: scenes of infant life in the nursery, such as "Pat-a-cake" and "The Children's Tea"; in the school-room, such as "Lessons"; and out of school hours, such as "Bubbles" and "The Children's Maypole." In one and all of these it is her own family who are the chief actors.

The portrayal of her children in heads of a larger size than her usual work was at this time seen by friends and others, who pressed upon her commissions for effigies of their own little ones, a branch of work which promptly drew down upon her the disapproval of Ruskin, who wrote: "I am indeed sorrowfully compelled to express my regret that she should have spent unavailing pains in finishing single heads, which are at the best uninteresting miniatures, instead of fulfilling her true gift, and doing what the Lord made her for in representing the gesture, character, and humour of charming children in country landscapes."

But this change naturally did not pass over her

work all at once, or even in a single year. Mrs.
Allingham's presentations of the countryside commenced in earnest shortly after her settling down at
Witley in 1881 ; but as will be seen by the dates of
the pictures which illustrate this chapter, the figure
as the dominant feature continues for another six
years ; in fact, during the whole of her seven and
a half years at Witley we find it now and again,
and do not part with it as such until 1890.   Since
then hardly a single example has come from her
brush.   Mrs. Allingham gives as her reason for
the change that she came to the conclusion that
she could put as much interest into a figure two
or three inches high as in one three times as large,
and that she could paint it better ; for in painting
large figures out of doors it was always a difficulty
in making them look anything else than they were,
namely, "posing models."

But if the figure ceases to occupy the foremost
position, it is still there, and is always present
to add a charming vitality to all that she does.
To people a landscape with figures, of captivating
mien, each taking its proper position, and each
adding to the interest of the whole, is a gift which
is the property of but few landscapists.   It is
indeed a gift, for we have before us the example

of the greatest landscapist of all, who the more he
strove the more he failed.   But it is a gift which
we believe many more might obtain by strenuous
endeavour.   It is always a matter of surprise to
the ignorant public how it comes to pass that an
artist who can draw nature admirably should never
attempt to learn the draftsmanship of the human
figure, by the omission of which from his work he
deprives it of half its interest and value.   He often
goes a step further, and shows not his inability but
his indolence by producing picture after picture,
upon the face of which no single instance occurs
of the introduction of man, beast, or bird, save
and except a single unpretentious creature of the
lowest grade of the feathered creation ; this, however, he will draw sufficiently well to prove that
he could, an he would, double the interest in his
landscapes.   To the outsider this appears incom-
prehensible in the person of those who apparently
are thorough artists, ardent in their profession.
One meets such an one at table, and even between
the courses he cannot refrain from taking out his
pencil and covering the menu with his scribblings ;
but the same man appears before Nature without a
note-book, in which he might be storing so many
jottings, which would be of untold value to his work.

Mrs. Allingham's case has been the entire contrary to this ; she has, I will not say toiled, for the garnering must be a pleasure, but stored, many a time and oft, for future use, a mass of valuable material, so that she is never at a loss for the right adjunct to fit the right place.   Her so doing was, in the first instance, due entirely to her husband. He said, truly, that the introduction of animals and birds, in fact, any form of life, gave scale and interest to a picture, and he urged her to begin making studies from the first.   There is not the slightest doubt that she owed very much to him that habit of thinking out fitting figures, as she has always tried, and with exceptional success, as accessories to every landscape.

Her sketch-books, consequently, are full not only of men, women, and children, and their immediate belongings, but of most of the animal life which follows in their train.   I say "most," because for some reason, which I have not elicited from her, she has preferences.   Horses, cattle, and sheep she will have but little of, only occasionally introducing them in distant hay or harvest fields.   The only instances of anything akin to either in this book are the animals in "The Goat Carriage," and "The Donkey Ride."   Nor will she have much to say to dogs, but for cats she has a great fondness, and they animate a large number of her scenes. Fowls, pigeons, and the like she paints to the life, and she apparently is thoroughly acquainted with their habits ; but other winged creatures, save an occasional robin, she avoids. Rabbits, wild and tame, she often introduces.

Her pictures being always typical of repose, she avoids much motion in her figures. Her children even, seldom indulge in violent action, unlike those of Birket Foster, who run races down hill, use the skipping-rope, fly kites, and urge the horses in the lane out of their accustomed foots-pace.

As typical examples of the drawings made in the early days at Witley, and whilst the figure was the main object, we have selected the following :—

23. THE CHILDREN'S TEA

From the Water-colour in the possession of Mr. W. Hollins.

Painted 1882.

This is the most important, and, to my mind, the most delightful of any of Mrs. Allingham's creations;

quite individual, and quite unlike the work of any one else.   Not only is the subject a charming one, but the actors in it all hold one's attention. It is certainly destined in the future to hold a high place among the examples of English water-colour art.

The scene is laid in Mrs. Allingham's dining-room at Sandhills, Witley, and contains portraits of her children.   The incidents are slight but original.   The mother is handing a cup of tea, but no one notices it, for the eldest girl's attention is taken up with the old cat lapping its milk, her younger sister, with her back to the window, is occupied in feeding her doll, propped up against a cup, from a large bowl of bread and milk, and the two other children are attracted to a sulphur butterfly which has just alighted on a glass of lilies of the valley.   The *etceteras* are painted as beautifully as the bigger objects; note, for instance, the bowl of daffodils on the old oak cupboard, the china on the table, and even the buns and the preserves. The whole is suffused with the warmth of a spring afternoon, the season being ascertainable by the budding trees outside, and the spring flowers inside. Exception may be taken to the faces not being more in shadow from a light which, although reflected from the tablecloth, is apparently behind them, and to the tablecloth being whiter than the sky, which it would not be. The fact, as regards the former, is that the faces were also lit from a window behind the spectator, whilst the latter is a permissible licence.

24. THE STILE

From the Water-colour in the possession of Mr. Alfred Shuttleworth.

Painted 1883.

The effort of negotiating a country stile, such as the one here depicted, which has no aids in the way of subsidiary steps, always induces a desire to rest by the way. Especially is this the case when a well-worn top affords a substantial seat. Time is evidently of little importance to the two sisters, for they have lingered in the hazel copse gathering hyacinths and primroses. Besides, the little one has asserted her right to a meal, and that would of itself be a sufficient excuse for lingering on the journey. The dog seems of the same way of thinking, and is evidently eagerly weighing the chances as to how much of the slice of bread and butter will fall to its share.

The drawing is a rich piece of colouring, but the hedgerow bank, with its profusion and variety of flowers, shows just that lack of a restraining hand which is so evident in Mrs. Allingham's fully-matured work. It was painted entirely in the open air, close to Sandhills, and the model who sat for the little child is now the artist's housemaid.

25. "PAT-A-CAKE"

From the Water-colour in the possession of Sir F. Wigan, Bt.

Painted 1884.

This drawing, although painted later than "The Children's Tea," would seem to be the prelude to a set in which practically the same figures take a part.

The motive here, as in all Mrs. Allingham's subjects, is of the simplest kind. The young girl reads from nursery rhymes that time-honoured one of "Pat-a-cake, Pat-a-cake, Baker's Man." It is apparently her younger brother's first introduction to the bye-play of patting, which should accompany its recitation, for the child regards the performance with some doubt, and has to be trained by the nurse as to how its hands should be manœuvred.

The drawing is full of details, such as the work-box, scissors, thimble, primroses, and anemones in the bowl, the china in the cupboard, and the coloured engraving on the wall, which, as we have seen in the case of other painters who have prac-tised it, opens up in fuller maturity a power of painting which is never possible to those who have neglected such an education.

26. LESSONS

From the Water-colour in the possession of Mr. C. P. Johnson.

Painted 1835.

The relations between the teacher and the taught appear to be somewhat strained this summer morning, for the little girl in pink is evidently at fault with her lessons, and the boy, while presum-ably figuring up a sum on his slate, has his eyes and ears open for a break in the silence which fills the room for the moment. However, in a short time it will be halcyon weather for all the actors, for the sun is streaming in at the window, the roses show that it is high summer, and a day on which the sternest teacher could not condemn the most intractable child to lengthy indoor imprisonment.

This drawing is of the same importance as regards size as "The Children's Tea," and is full of charm in every part.

27. BUBBLES

From the Water-colour in the possession of Mr. H. B. Beaumont.

Painted 1886.

Lessons are over, a stool has been brought from the schoolroom, the kitchen has been invaded, and the dish of soapsuds having been placed upon it the fun has begun. Who, that has enjoyed it, will forget the acrid taste of the long new churchwarden (where do the children of the present day find such pipes if they ever condescend to the fascinating game of bubble-blowing?) that one naturally sucked away at long before the watery compound was ready, the still more pungent taste of the household soap, the delight of seeing the first iridescent globe detach itself from the pipe and float upwards on the still air, or of raising a hundred globules by blowing directly into the basin, as the smocked youngster is doing here. Such joys countervailed the smarts which befell one's eyes when the burst bubble scattered its fragments into them, or when the suds came to an end, not through their dissipation into air, but over one's clothes.

28. ON THE SANDS—SANDOWN, ISLE OF WIGHT

From the Water-colour in the possession of Mrs. Francis Black.

Painted about 1886.

The family of young children that was now growing up round our artist naturally necessitated the summer holiday assuming a visit to the seaside, and much of Mrs. Allingham's time was, no doubt, spent on the shore in their company. It is little matter for surprise that this pleasure was combined with that of welding them into pictures; and, if an excuse must be made for Mrs. Allingham oftentimes robing her little girls in pink, it is to be found in the fact that the models were almost invariably her own children, who were so attired. It certainly will not be one of the least agreeable incidents for those who saunter over the illustrations of this volume to distinguish them and trace their growth from the cradle onwards, until they pass out of the stage of child models.

This drawing was painted on the shore at Sandown, Isle of Wight, where the detritus of the

Culver chalk cliffs afforded, in combination with
the sand, splendid material for the early achievements in architecture and estate planning which
used to yield so healthy an occupation to
youngsters.

It was a hazardous task to attempt success with
such a variety of tones of white as here presented
themselves, but the result is entirely satisfactory.
In fact the drawing shows how readily and with
what success the painter took up another phase of
outdoor work, not easy of accomplishment. In
those collections which include these seashore
subjects they single themselves out from all their
neighbours by the aptitude with which figures and
a limpid sea are painted in sunshine. This, again,
is no doubt due to their having been entirely out-
of-doors work.

29. DRYING CLOTHES

From the Water-colour in the possession of Mr. C. P. Johnson.

Painted 1886.

This important drawing, in which the figure is
on a large scale, makes one regret that Mrs.
Allingham abandoned her portraiture, for a more

captivating life study it is hard to imagine. Flattery apart, one may say that Frederick Walker never drew a more ideal figure or conceived a more charming colour scheme. The only feature which would perhaps have been omitted from a later work is that of the foxgloves in the corner, which appears to be rather an artificial introduction. The note of the little child behind the gate is charming. It is evidently not allowed to wander in the field, although the well-worn path shows that here is the main road to the cottage, and it feels that a joy is denied it not to be allowed to participate in the ceremony of gathering in of the family washing, as it was in younger days when the clothes were hung out.

30. HER MAJESTY'S POST OFFICE

From the Water-colour in the possession of Mr. H. B. Beaumont.

Painted 1887.

This, at the time it was painted, was the only Post Office of which Bowler's Green, near Hasle-mere, boasted, and from its appearance it might well have served during the reigns of several of Her Majesty's predecessors. It speaks much for the

absence of ill-disposed persons in the neighbourhood that letters were for so long entrusted to its
care, as it seems far removed from the days of the
scarlet funnel which probably now replaces it. I
opine that the young gentleman whom we saw a
short while ago engaged in bubble-blowing has
been entrusted here with the posting of a letter.

31. THE CHILDREN'S MAYPOLE

From the Water-colour in the possession of Mrs. Dobson.

Painted 1886.

May Day still lingers in some parts of the
country, for only last year in an out-of-the-way
lane in Northamptonshire the writer encountered a
band of children decked in flowers, and their best
frocks and ribbons, singing an old May ditty. But
lovers have long ago ceased to plant trees before
their mistresses' doors, and to dance with them
afterwards round the maypole on the village green,
which we too are old enough to remember in
Leicestershire. The ceremony that Mrs. Allingham's children are taking a part in was doubtless
the recognition by a poet of his illustrious pre-
decessor Spenser's exhortation :—

Youths folke now flocken in everywhere
To gather May baskets, and smelling briere ;
And home they hasten, the postes to dight
With hawthorne buds, and sweet eglantine,
And girlonds of roses, and soppes in wine.

The scene is laid in the woods at Witley.

CHAPTER VI

THE WOODS, THE LANES, AND THE FIELDS

I've been dreaming all night, and thinking all day, of the hedge-
    rows of England ;
They are in blossom now, and the country is all like a garden ;
Thinking of lanes and of fields, and the song of the lark and the
    linnet.

WHEN Mrs. Allingham finally, I will not say
determined to cut herself away from figure painting, but by the influence of her surroundings
drifted away from it, she did not, as so many do,
become the delineator of a single phase of landscape art. Her journeyings in search of subjects
for some years were neither many nor extensive,
for a paintress with a family growing up around
her has not the same opportunities as a painter.
He can leave his incumbrances in charge of his
wife, and his work will probably benefit by an
occasional flitting from home surroundings. But

a mother's work would not thrive away from her children even if absence was possible, which it probably was not in Mrs. Allingham's case. Hence we find that the ground she has covered has been almost entirely confined to what are termed the Home Counties, with an occasional diversion to the Isle of Wight, Dorsetshire, Gloucestershire, and Cheshire. In the Home Counties, Surrey and Kent have furnished most of her material, the former naturally being oftenest drawn upon during her life at Witley, and the latter since she lived in London, whither she returned in the year 1888. This inability to roam about whither she chose was doubtless helpful in compelling her to vary her subjects, for she would of necessity have to paint whatever came within her reach. But her energy also had its share, for it enabled her to search the whole countryside wherever she was, and gather in a dozen suitable scenes where another might only discover one.

As evidence of this we may instance the case of the corner of Kent whither she has gone again and again of late, and where in the present year she has still been able to find ample material to her liking. A visit to this somewhat out-of-the-way spot, which lies in Kent in an almost identically similar position to that which Witley does in Surrey, namely, in the extreme south-west corner, shows how she has found material everywhere. In the mile that separates the station from the farmhouse where she encamps, she shows a cottage that she has painted from every side, a brick kiln that she has her eye on, an old yew, and a clump of elms that has been most serviceable. Arriving at the farm-gate she points to the modest floral display in front that has sufficed for " In the Farmhouse Garden " (Plate 2), whilst over the way are the buildings of " A Kentish Farmyard " (Plate 58). Entering the house the visitor may not be much impressed with the view from her sitting-room window, but under the artist's hands it has become the silvern sheet of daisies reproduced in Plate 38. " On the Pilgrims' Way " (Plate 41) is a field or so away, whilst a short walk up the downs behind the house finds us in the presence of the originals of Plates 32 and 36. A drive across the vale and we have Crockham Hill, whence comes Plate 40, and Ide Hill, Plate 55.

A ramble round these scenes, whilst a most enjoyable matter to any one born to an apprecia-tion of the country, was in truth not the inspiration that would be imagined to the writer of the text, for he had seen, for instance, the daintily conceived water-colour of "Ox-eye Daisies" (Plate 38), painted a year ago, and he arrived at the field to find this year's crop a failure, and on a day in which the distant woods were hardly visible; the scene of the "Foxgloves" had all the underwood grown up, and only a stray spike suggestive of the glory of past years; gipsy tramps on the road to "berrying" (strawberry gathering) conjured up no visions of the tenant of Mrs. Allingham's "Spring on the Kentish Downs," but only a horrible thought of the strawberries defiled by being picked by their hands.

This description of the variety of the artist's work within a single small area will show that it is somewhat difficult to classify it for consideration. However, one or two arrangements and rearrangements of the drawings which illustrate these phases of the artist's output seem to bring them best into the following divisions: woods, lanes, and fields; cottages; and gardens. These we shall therefore consider in this and the following chapters, dealing here with the first of them.

Midway in her life at Witley, The Fine Art Society induced Mrs. Allingham to undertake, as the subject for an Exhibition, the portrayal of the countryside under its four seasonal aspects of spring,

summer, autumn, and winter. She completed her
task, and the result was shown in 1886 in an
Exhibition, but a glance at the catalogue shows in
which direction her preference lay ; for whilst spring
and summer between them accounted for more than
fifty pictures, only seven answered for autumn, and
six, of which one half were interiors, illustrated
winter. These proportions may not perhaps have
represented the ratio of her affections, but of her
physical ability to portray each of the seasons.
Autumn leaves and tints no doubt appealed to her
artistic eye as much as spring or summer hues, but
for some reason, perhaps that of health, illustrations
were few and far between of the time of year

> When yellow leaves, or none, or few, do hang
> Upon those boughs which shake against the cold,
> Bare ruin'd choirs, where late the sweet birds sang.

In so selecting she differed from Mr. Ruskin,
who has laid it down that " a tree is never meant
to be drawn with all its leaves on, any more than a
day when its sun is at noon. One draws the day
in its morning or eventide, the tree in its spring
or autumn dress." This naturally exaggerated
dictum is the contrary of Mrs. Allingham's practice.
She almost invariably waits for the trees until they

34. SPRING IN THE OAKWOOD

35. THE CUCKOO

36. THE OLD YEW TREE

37. THE HAWTHORN VALLEY, BROCKET

38. OX-EYE DAISIES, NEAR WESTERHAM, KENT

39. FOXGLOVES

40. HEATHER ON CROCKHAM HILL, KENT

41. ON THE PILGRIM'S WAY

42. NIGHT-JAR LANE, WITLEY

43. CHERRY-TREE COTTAGE, CHIDDINGFOLD

44. COTTAGE AT CHIDDINGFOLD

45. A COTTAGE AT HAMBLEDON

46. IN WORMLEY WOOD

47. THE ELDER BUSH, BROOK LANE, WITLEY

48. THE BASKET WOMAN

49. COTTAGE AT SHOTTERMILL, NEAR HASLEMERE

have completely donned their spring garb, and leaves them ere they doff their summer dress.

The drawings of the woods, lanes, and fields which Mrs. Allingham has selected for illustration here comprise six of spring, three of summer, and two of autumn, winter being unrepresented. They are culled as to seven from Kent, three from Surrey, and a single one from Hertfordshire.

Taking them in their seasonal order we may discuss them as follows :—

32. SPRING ON THE KENTISH DOWNS

From the Water-colour in the possession of Mrs. Beddington.

Painted 1900.

Out of the city, far away
With spring to-day !
Where copses tufted with primrose
Give one repose.

WILLIAM ALLINGHAM.

That the joy of spring is a never-failing subject for poets, any one may see who turns over the pages of the numerous compilations which now treat of Nature. I doubt, however, whether they receive a higher pleasure from it than does the townsman who can only walk afield at rare intervals, and whose first visit to the country each year is taken at Eastertide. He probably has no eye save for the contrasts which he experiences to his daily life, of scene, air, and vitality, but these will certainly infect him with a healthier love of life than is enjoyed by those who live amongst them and see them come and go.

Fortunate is the man who can visit these Kentish downs at a time when the breath of spring is touching everything, when the eastern air makes one appreciate the shelter that the hazel copses fringing their sides afford, an appreciation which is shared by the firs which hug their southern slopes.

It is very early spring in this drawing. The highest trees show no sign of it save at their outermost edges. Hazels alone, and they only in the shelter, have shed their flowery tassels, and assumed a leafage which is still immature in colour. The sprawling trails of the traveller's joy, which rioted over everything last autumn, are still without any trace of returning vitality.

33. TIG BRIDGE

From the Water-colour in the possession of Mr. E. S. Curwen.

Painted 1887.

Here the white ray'd anemone is born,
Wood-sorrel, and the varnish'd buttercup;
And primrose in its purfled green swathed up,
Pallid and sweet round every budding thorn.

WILLIAM ALLINGHAM.

This little sequestered bridge would hardly seem to be of sufficient importance to deserve a name, nor for the matter of that the streamlet, the Tigbourne, which runs beneath it, but on the Hindhead slope streams of any size are scarce, and therefore call for notice. Bridges resemble stiles in being enforced loitering places, for whilst there is no effort which compels a halt in crossing bridges, as there is with stiles, there is the sense of mystery which underlies them, and expectancy as to what the water may contain. Especially is this so for youth; and so here we have boy and girl who pause on their way from bluebell gathering, whilst the former makes belief of fishing with the thread of twine which youngsters of his age always find to hand in one or other of their pockets.

34. SPRING IN THE OAKWOOD

From the Water-colour in the possession of the Artist.

Painted 1903.

We have elsewhere remarked on the rare occa
sions on which Mrs. Allingham utilises sunlight
and shadow. Here, however, is one of them, and
one which shows that it is from no incapacity to
do so, for it is now introduced with a difficult
effect, namely, blue flowers under a low raking
light. The artist's eye was doubtless attracted by
the unusual visitation of a bright warm sun on a
spring day, and determined to perpetuate it.

The wood in which the scene is laid is on the
Kentish Downs, where, as the distorted boughs
show, the winds are always in evidence.

The juxtaposition of the two primaries, blue
and yellow, is always a happy one in nature, but
specially is it so when we have such a mass of
sapphire blue.

> Blue, gentle cousin of the forest green,
> Married to green in all the sweetest flowers—
> Forget-me-not, the bluebell, and that queen
> Of secrecy the violet.

35. THE CUCKOO

From the Water-colour in the possession of Mr. A. Hugh Thompson.

Painted about 1887.

In a recent " One Man Exhibition" by that refined artist Mr. Eyre Walker, there was a very unusual drawing entitled " Beauty for Ashes." The entire foreground was occupied with a luxuriant growth of purple willow loosestrife, intermixed with the silvery white balls of down from seeding nipplewort. Standing gaunt from this intermingling, luxuriant crop, were the charred stems of burnt fir trees, whilst the living mass of their fellows formed an agreeable background. The subject must have attracted many travellers on the South-Western Railway as they passed Byfleet; it did so in Mr. Walker's case to the extent that he stayed his journey and painted it.

In that case this beautiful display had, as the title to the picture hints, arisen from the ashes of a forest. A spark from a train had set fire to the wood, and had apparently destroyed every living thing in its course. But such is Nature that out of death sprang life. So it has been with the coppice here, and in the oakwood scene which preceded it. The cutting down and clearing of the wood has brought sun, air, and rain to the soil, and as a consequence have followed the

> Sheets of hyacinth
> That seem the heavens upbreaking thro' the earth.

The drawing takes its name from the cuckoo whose note has arrested the children's attention.

36. THE OLD YEW TREE

From the Water-colour in the possession of the Artist.

Painted 1903.

> The sad yew is seen
> Still with the black cloak round his ancient wrongs.
>
> WILLIAM ALLINGHAM.

One of many that are dotted about the southern slopes of the Westerham Downs, and that, not only here but all along the line of the Pilgrims' Way, are regarded as having their origin in these devotees. The drawing was made in the early part of the present year, when the primroses and violets were out, but before there was anything else, save the blossom of the willow, to show that

> The spring comes slowly up this way,
>   Slowly, slowly!
> To give the world high holiday.

37. THE HAWTHORN VALLEY, BROCKET

From the Water-colour in the possession of Lord Mount-Stephen.

Painted 1898.

It is somewhat remarkable that the most impressive flower-show that Nature presents to our notice, namely, when, as May passes into June, the whole countryside is decked with a bridal array of pure white, should have taken hold of but few of our poets.

Shakespeare, of course, recognised it in lines which make one smile at the idea that they could ever have been composed by a town-bred poet ·—

> O what a life were this! How sweet, how lovely!
> Gives not the hawthorn-bush a sweeter shade
> To shepherds, looking on their silly sheep,
> Than doth a rich embroidered canopy
> To kings that fear their subjects' treachery.

Another, in the person of Mrs. Allingham's husband, penned a sonnet upon it containing the following happy description :—

> Cluster'd pearls upon a robe of green,
> And broideries of white bloom.

The scene of this drawing is laid in the park at Brocket Hall, to which reference is made in con-

nection with a subsequent illustration (Plate 65).
The park is full of ancient timber, one great oak on
the border of the two counties (Herts and Beds)
being mentioned in Doomsday Book, and another
going by the name of Queen Elizabeth's oak, from
the tradition that the Princess was sitting under it
when the news reached her that she was Queen of
England.[1]   The Hawthorn Valley runs for nearly
a mile from one of the park entrances towards the
more woodland part of the estate, and was formerly
used as a private race-course.

The artist has treated a very difficult subject
with success, as any one, especially an amateur,
who has tried to portray masses of hawthorn
blossom will readily admit.   Any attempt to draw
the flowers and fill in the foliage is hopeless, and
it can only be done, as in this case, by erasure.
Hardly less difficult to accomplish are the delicate
fronds of the young bracken, unfolding upwards by
inches a day, which can only be treated suggestively.
In the original, which is on a somewhat large scale,
the middle distance is enlivened with browsing
rabbits, but the very considerable reduction of the
drawing has reduced these to a size which renders
them hardly distinguishable.

[1] Another tree at Hatfield also claims this distinction.

38. OX-EYE DAISIES, NEAR WESTERHAM, KENT

From the Water-colour in the possession of the Artist.

Painted 1902.

Whilst no Exhibition passes nowadays which has not one or more representations of the " blithe populace " of daisies, the fashion has only come in of late years.   Even the Flemings, who were so partial to the flowers of the field, seem to have considered it beneath their notice—a strange occurrence, because one can hardly turn over the pages of any missal of a corresponding epoch without coming upon many a faithful representation of the rose-encircled orb.

Chaucer extolled it

> Above all the flow'res in the mead
> Then love I most these flow'res white and red,
> Such that men callen daisies in our town.

And much content it gave him

> To see this flow'r against the sunne spread.
> When it upriseth early by the morrow
> That blissful sight softeneth all my sorrow.

He recognised its name of " day's eye," because it opens and closes its flower with the daylight, in the lines—

> The daisie or els the eye of the daie,
> The emprise and the floure of floures alle.

In fact it was a favourite with English poets long
before it came under the notice of English painters.
Witness Milton's well-known line—

Meadows trim with daisies pied.

It was not until the epoch of the pre-Raphaelite
brethren that the daisies which pie the meadows
seemed worthy of perpetuation, and it was reserved
to Frederick Walker, in his " Harbour of Refuge,"
to limn them on a lawn falling beneath the scythe.

The flower that Mrs. Allingham has painted
with so much skill—for it is a very difficult under-
taking to suggest a mass of daisies without too much
individualising—is not, of course, the field daisy
(*bellis perennis*) but the ox-eye, or moon daisy,
which is really a chrysanthemum (*chrysanthemum
leucanthemum*), a plant which seems to have increased very much of late years, especially on railway embankments, maybe because it has come into
vogue, and actually been advanced to a flower
worthy of gathering and using as a table decoration,
an honour that would never have been bestowed
on it a quarter of a century ago.

The drawing was made from the window of the
farmhouse in Kent, to which, as we have said,
Mrs. Allingham runs down at all seasons.   It was

evidently made on a glorious summer day, when
every flower had expanded to its utmost under the
delicious heat of a ripening sun.   The bulbous
cloudlet which floats in front of the whiter strata,
and the blueness of the distant woods may augur
rain in the near future, but for the moment everything appears to be in a serenely happy condition,
except perhaps the farmer, who would fain see a
crop in which there was less flower and more grass.

39. FOXGLOVES

From the Water-colour in the possession of Mrs. C. A. Barton.

Painted 1898.

Foxgloves have appealed to Mrs. Allingham for
portrayal in more than one locality in England,
but never in greater luxuriance than on this Kentish
woodside, where their spikes overtop the sweet
little sixteen-year-old faggot-carrier.   It happens
to be another instance of a magnificent crop spring-
ing up the first year after a growth of saplings have
been cleared away, and not to be repeated even in
this year of grace (1903) when the newspapers have
been full of descriptions of the unwonted displays
of foxgloves everywhere, and have been taunting

the gardeners upon their poor results in comparison with Nature's.

40. HEATHER ON CROCKHAM HILL, KENT

From the Water-colour in the possession of the Artist.

Painted 1902.

It is perhaps a fallacy, or at least heresy, to assert that English heather bears away the palm for beauty over that of the country with which it is more popularly associated. But many, I am sure, will agree with me that nowhere in Scotland is any stretch of heather to be found which can eclipse in its magnificence of colour that which extends for mile after mile over Surrey and Kentish commonland in mid August. In the summer in which this drawing was painted it was especially noticeable as being in more perfect bloom than it had been known to be for many seasons.

41. ON THE PILGRIMS' WAY

From the Water-colour in the possession of the Artist.

Painted 1902.

I was taken to task by Mrs. Allingham a while ago for saying that her affections were not so set upon the delineation of harvesting as were those of most landscapists, and she stated that she had painted the sheafed fields again and again. But I held to my assertion, and proof comes in this drawing just handed to me. Not one artist in ten would, I am certain, have sat down to his subject on this side of the hedge, but would have been over the stile, and made his foreground of the shorn field and stacked sheaves, breaking their monotony of form and colour by the waggon and its attendant labourers. But Mrs. Allingham could not pass the harvest of the hedge, and was satisfied with just a peep of the corn through the gap formed by the stile. It is not surprising, for who that is fond of flowers could pass such a gladsome sight as the display which Nature has so lavishly offered month after month the summer through to those who cared to notice it. In May the hedge was white with hawthorn, in June gay with dog-roses and white briar, in July with convolvuli and woodbine, and now again in August comes the clematis and the blackberry flower.

42. NIGHT-JAR LANE, WITLEY

From the Drawing in the possession of Mr. E. S. Curwen.

Painted 1887.

One of those steep self-made roads which the passage of the seasons rather than of man has furrowed and deepened in "the flow of the deep still wood," a lodgment for the leaves from whose depths that charming lament of the dying may well have arisen,—

Said Fading Leaf to Fallen Leaf,
" I toss alone on a forsaken tree,
It rocks and cracks with every gust that rocks
Its straining bulk : say ! how is it with thee?"

Said Fallen Leaf to Fading Leaf,
" A heavy foot went by, an hour ago ;
Crush'd into clay, I stain the way ;
The loud wind calls me, and I cannot go."

The name "Night-Jar," by which this lane is known, is unusual, and probably points to its having been a favourite hunting-ground for a seldom-seen visitant, for which it seems well-fitted. The name may well date back to White of Selborne's time, who lived not far away, and termed the bird "a wonderful and curious creature," which it must be if, as he records, it commences its jar, or note, every evening so exactly at the close of day that it coincided to a second with the report—which he could distinguish in summer—of the Portsmouth evening gun.

Night-jars are most deceptive in their flight, one or two giving an illusion of many by their extremely rapid movements and turns; and they may well have been very noticeable to persons in the confined space of this gully, especially as the observer in his evening stroll would probably stir up the moths, which are the bird's favourite food, and which would attract it into his immediate vicinity. How much interest would be added to a countryside were the lanes all fitted with titles such as this.

CHAPTER VII

COTTAGES AND HOMESTEADS

The ancient haunts of men have numberless tongues for those who know how to hear them speak.

I was not until some fifteen years of Mrs. Allingham's career as a painter in water-colour had been accomplished that she found the subject with which her name has since been so inseparably linked. Looking through the ranks of her associates in the Art it is in rare instances that we encounter so complete a departure out of a long-practised groove, or one which has been so amply justified. But in selecting English Cottages and Homesteads, and peopling them with a comely tenantry, she happened upon a theme that was certain not only to obtain the suffrages of the ordinary exhibition visitors, but of those who add to seeing, admiration and acquisition. Thus it has come to pass that in the other fifteen years which have elapsed since she first began to paint them, " Mrs. Allingham's Cottages " have become a household word amongst connoisseurs of English water-colours, and no representative collection has been deemed to be complete without an example of them.

This appreciation is very assuredly a sound one, as the value of these pictures does not consist solely in their beauty as works of Art, but in their recording in line and colour a most interesting but unfortunately vanishing phase of English domestic architecture.   For the cottages are almost without exception veritable portraits, the artist (whilst naturally selecting those best suited to her purpose) having felt it a duty to present them with an accuracy of structural feature which is not always the case in creations of this kind, where the painter has had other views, and considered that he could improve his picture by an addition here and an omission there.

So many of Mrs. Allingham's drawings of cottages have been taken from the counties of Surrey and Sussex, that it may interest not only the owners of those here reproduced, but others who possess similar subjects, to read a short description of the features that distinguish the buildings in these districts.

One is perhaps too apt to pass these lowlier habitations of our fellow-men, whether we see them in reality or in their counterfeits, without a thought as to their structure, or an idea that it is an evolution which has grown on very marked lines from primitive types, and which in almost every instance has been influenced by local surroundings.

In the early days of housebuilding the use of local materials was naturally a distinctive feature of dwellings of every kind, but more especially in those where expenditure had to be kept within narrow limits. But even in such a case the style of architecture affected in the better built houses influenced and may be traced in the more humble ones. Change amongst our forefathers was even less hastily assumed than in these days, and a style which experience had proved to be convenient was persevered in for generation after generation, individuality seldom having any play, although a necessary adaptation to the site gave to most buildings a distinction of their own. One of the earliest forms, and one still to be found even in buildings which have now descended to the use of yeomen's dwellings, was that of a large central

room having on one side of it the smaller living
and sleeping rooms, and on the other the kitchens
and servants' apartments, the wings projecting
sometimes both to back and front, sometimes only
to the latter.   In later times, as such a house fell
into less well-to-do hands, necessity usually compelled the splitting-up of the house into various
tenements, in which event the central room was
generally divided into compartments, often into a
complete dwelling.   Types of this kind may be
found in most villages in the south-eastern counties,
and examples will be seen in "The Six Bells"
(Plate 57) and the house at West Tarring, near
Worthing (Plate 51), where the central portion
falls back from the gabled ends.   This arrangement
of a central hall used for a living room, after going
out of favour for some centuries, is curiously
enough once more coming into fashion.

Local materials having, as we have said, much
to do with the structure, the type of dwelling that
we may expect to find in counties where wood was
plentiful, and the cost of preparing and putting it
on the ground less than that of quarrying, shaping,
and carrying stone, is the picturesque, timber-
formed cottage.   Those interested in the plan of
construction, which was always simple, of these

will find full details in **Mr. Guy Dawber's** Introduction to *Old Cottages and Farm Houses in
Kent and Sussex,* as well as many illustrations of
examples that occur in these counties.

The materials other than wood used for the
framework, and which were necessary to fill up the
interstices, were, in the better class of dwellings,
bricks ; in others, a consistency formed of chopped
straw and clay, an outward symmetry of appearance being gained by a covering of plaster where
it was not deemed advisable to protect the wood-
work, and of boarding or tiles where the whole
surface called for protection.   Several of the
cottages illustrated in this volume have been pro-
tected by these tilings on some part or another,
perhaps only on a gable end, most often on the
upper story, sometimes over the whole building,
but of course, principally, where it **was** most ex-
posed to the weather (see Cherry-Tree Cottage,
Plate 43 ; Chiddingfold, Plate 44 ; Shottermill,
Plate 49 ; and Valewood Farm, Plate 50).   This
purpose of the tile in the old houses, and its use
only for protection, distinguishes them from the
modern erections, where it is oftentimes affixed in
the most haphazard style, and clearly without any
idea of fitting it where it will be most serviceable.

The space in the interior was very irregularly apportioned, whilst the cubic space allotted to living rooms, both on the ground and first floors, was singularly insufficient for modern hygienic views. A reason for the small size of the rooms may have been that it enabled them to be more readily warmed, either by the heat given off by the closely-packed indwellers, or by the small wood fires which alone could be indulged in. Little use was made of the large space in the roof, but this omission adds much to the picturesqueness of the exterior, for the roofs gain in simplicity by their unbroken surface and treatment. It is somewhat astonishing that the old builders did not recognise this costly disregard of space.

The roofs, like the framework, testify to the geological formation and agricultural conditions of the district.

The roof-tree was always of hand-hewn oak, and this it was, according to Birket Foster, which gave to many of the old roofs their pleasant curves away from the central chimney. The ordinary unseasoned sawn deal of the modern roof may swag in any direction.

The roof-covering where the land was chiefly arable, or the distance from market considerable,

was usually wheaten thatch, which was certainly
the most comfortable, being warm in winter and
cool in summer, just the reverse of the tiles or
slates that have practically supplanted it.[1]   In
other districts the cottages are covered with what
are known as stone slates, thick and heavy.   Roofs
to carry the weight of these had always to be
flattened, with the result that they require mor-
taring to keep out the wet.   The West Tarring
cottage (Plate 51) is an instance of a stone roofing.

The red tiles, which were used for the most part,
are certainly the most agreeable to the artistic eye,
for their seemingly haphazard setting, due in part
to the builder and in part to nature, affords that
pleasure which always arises from an unstudied
irregularity of line.   Roof tiles were made thicker

---

[1] See " In Wormley Wood " (Plate 46), in the description of which
I have referred to the reasons for the disappearance of thatch as a roof
material.   An additional one to those there mentioned is without doubt
the risk of fire.   Since the introduction of coal, chimneys clog much
more readily with soot, and a fire from one of these with its showers of
sparks may quickly set ablaze not only the cottage where this happens,
but the whole village.   That the insurance companies, by their higher
premiums for thatch-covered houses, recognise a greater risk, may or
may not be proof of greater liability to conflagration, but we certainly
nowadays hear of much fewer of those disasters, which even persons
now living can remember, whereby whole villages were swept out of
existence.

and less carefully in the old days, and our artist's truth in delineation may be detected in almost any drawing by examining where the weight has swagged away the tiles between the main roof beams.

Unlike chimneys erected by our cottage builders of to-day, which appear to issue out of a single mould, those of the untutored architects of the past present every variety of treatment and appearance.

The old solidly built chimney seen in many of Mrs. Allingham's cottages (Chiddingfold, Plate 44) is worthy of note as a type of many sturdy fellows which have resisted the ravages of time, and have stood for centuries almost without need of repair. In old days the chimney was regarded not only as a special feature but as an ornament, and not as a necessary but ugly excrescence. Although probably it only served for one room in the house, that service was an important one, and so materials were liberally used in its construction.

In Kent and Sussex many of the chimneys are of brick, although the house and the base of the chimney-stack are of stone. This arose from the stone not lending itself to thin slabs, and

consequently being altogether too cumbrous and
bulky.

The windows in the old cottages were naturally
small when glass was a luxury, and became fewer
in number when a tax upon light was one of the
means for carrying on the country's wars. They
were usually filled with the smallest panes, fitted
into lead lattice, so that breakages might be reduced
to the smallest area. Not much of this remains,
but a specimen of it is to be seen in the Old Buckinghamshire House (Plate 52). One of the few
alterations that Mrs. Allingham allows herself is the
substitution of these diamond lattices throughout
a house where she finds a single example in any of
the lights, or if, as she has on more than one
occasion found, that they have been replaced by
others, and are themselves stacked up as rubbish.
She has in her studio some that have been served in
this way, and which have now become useful models.

It would be imagined that the sense of pride in
these, the last traces of their village ancestors,
would have prompted their descendants, whether
of the same kin or not, to deal reverently with them,
and endeavour to hand on as long as possible these
silent witnesses to the honest workmanship of their
forbears. Such, unfortunately, is but seldom the

case. If any one will visit Witley with this book
in his hand, and compare the present state of the
few examples given there, not twenty years after
they were painted, he will see what is taking
place not only in this little village but through
the length and breadth of England. It is not
always wilful on the part of the landlord, but
arises from either his lack of sympathy, time, or
interest.

He probably has a sense of his duty to "keep
up" things, and so sends his agent to go round
with an architect and settle a general plan for
doing up the old places (usually described as
"tumbling down" or "falling to pieces"). Thereupon a village builder makes an estimate and sends
in a scratch pack of masons and joiners, and between
them they often supplant fine old work, most of it
as firm as a rock, with poor materials and careless
labour, and rub out a piece of old England, irre-
coverable henceforth by all the genius in the world
and all the money in the bank. The drainage and
water supply, points where improvement is often
desirable, may be left unattended to. But whatever else is decided on, no uneven tiled roofs,
with moss and houseleek, must remain ; no thatch
on any pretence, nor ivy on the wall, nor vine along

the eaves.   The cherry or apple tree, that pushed
its blossoms almost into a lattice, will probably be
cut down, and the wild rose and honeysuckle hedge
be replaced by a row of pales or wires.   The
leaden lattice itself and all its fellows, however
perfect, must inevitably give place to a set of
mean little square windows of unseasoned wood,
though perhaps on the very next property an
architect is building imitation old cottages with
lattices ! With the needful small repairs, most of
the real old cottages would have lasted for many
generations to come, to the satisfaction of their
inhabitants and the delight of all who can feel the
charm of beauty combined with ancientness—a
charm once lost, lost for ever.   And unquestionably
the well-repaired old cottages would generally be
more comfortable than the new or the done-up
ones, to say nothing of the "sentiment" of the
cottager.   An old man, who was in a temporary
lodging during the doing-up of his cottage, being
asked, "When shall you get back to your house ?"
answered, "In about a month, they tells me ; but
it won't be like going home."   At the same time
it is fair to add that many of the "doings-up" in
Mrs. Allingham's country are of good intention
and less ruthless execution than may be seen else-

where, and that certain owners show a real feeling of wise conservatism. It would perhaps be a low estimate, however, to say that a thousand ancient cottages are now disappearing in England every twelvemonth, without trace or record left—many that Shakespeare might have seen, some Chaucer; while the number "done up" is beyond computation.

The baronial halls have had abundant recognition and laudation at the hands of the historian and the painter; the numerous manor-houses, less pretentious, often more lovely, very little; the old cottages next to none, even the local chronicler running his spectacles over them without a pause.

It really looks as if we were, one and all, constituted as a poet has seen us :—

> For, don't you mark, we're made so that we love
> First when we see them painted, things we have passed
> Perhaps a hundred times nor cared to see;
> And so they are better, painted—better to us,
> Which is the same thing.   Art was given for that—
> God uses us to help each other so,
> Lending our minds out.

Had Mrs. Allingham done nothing else for her country, she has justified her career as a recorder of this altogether overlooked phase of English architecture—a phase which will soon be a thing of the past.

I remember once being accosted by a bystander in Angers, as I was wrestling with the perspective of a beautiful old house, with the remark, " Ah, you had better hurry more than you are doing and finish the roof of that house, for it will be off to-morrow and the whole down in three days." That has often been the case with Mrs. Allingham. More than once a cottage limned one summer has disappeared before the drawing was exhibited the following spring. Year in and year out the process has been at work during the quarter of a century during which the artist has been garnering, and it has almost come to be a joke that were she to paint as long again as she has, she might have to cease from actual lack of material.

Our illustrations of cottages divide themselves into, first the examples in the immediate neigh-bourhood of Sandhills ; and secondly, those farther afield in Kent, Buckingham, Dorset, the Isle of Wight, and Cheshire.

Those near Sandhills form points in the circumference of a circle of which it is the centre, the most southern being Chiddingfold, where we start on our survey.

43. CHERRY-TREE COTTAGE, CHIDDINGFOLD

From the Water-colour in the possession of the
Lord Chief Justice of England.

Painted 1885.

The old hamlet of Chiddingfold lies about as far to the south as Witley does to the north of the station on the London and South-Western Railway which bears their joint names. It boasts of a very ancient inn, "The Crown,"—formed, it is said, in part out of a monastic building,—and a large village green. Cherry-Tree Cottage is, as will be seen, the milk shop of the place, and, if we may judge from the coming and going in Mrs. Alling ham's picture, carries on an animated, prosperous trade at certain times of the day.

44. COTTAGE AT CHIDDINGFOLD

From the Water-colour in the possession of Mr. H. L. Florence.

Painted 1889.

We have here a March day, or rather one of the type associated with that month, but which

usually visits us with increasing severity as April
and May and the summer progress. Wind in the
east, with the sky a cold, steely blue in the zenith,
greying even the young elm shoots a stone's-throw
distant. The cottage almanack, Old Moore's, will
foretell that night frosts will prevail, and the
cottager will be fearsome of its effect upon his
apple crop, always so promising in its blossom, so
scanty in its fulfilment. Splendid weather for the
full-blooded lassies, who can tarry to gossip without
fear of chills, and also for drying clothes on the
hedgerow, but nipping for the old beldame who
tends them, and who has to wrap up against it
with shawl and cap.

> Laburnum, rich
> In streaming gold,

competes in colour with the spikes of the broom,
which the artist must have been thankful to the
hedgecutter for sparing as he passed his shears
along its surface when last he trimmed it. For
some reason the broom bears an ill repute hereabouts as bringing bad luck, although in early
times it was put to a desirable use, as Gerard tells
us that "that worthy Prince of famous memory,
Henry VIII. of England, was wont to drink the

distilled water of Broome floures." Wordsworth
also gives it [1] a special word in his lines—

> Am I not
> In truth a favour'd plant?
> On me such bounty summer showers,
> That I am cover'd o'er with flowers;
> And when the frost is in the sky,
> My branches are so fresh and gay,
> That you might look on me and say—
> "This plant can never die."

The cottage contains a typical example of the
massive central chimney, and also an end one,
which it is unusual to find in company with the
other in so small a dwelling. Note also the weather
tiling round the gable end and the upper story.

45. A COTTAGE AT HAMBLEDON

From the Water-colour in the possession of Mr. F. Pennington.

Painted 1888.

For those who read between the lines there are
plenty of pretty allegories connected with these
drawings. This, for instance, might well be termed
"Youth and Age." The venerable cottage in its
declining years, so appropriately set in a framework

[1] Do not these lines rather refer to gorse?

of autumn tints and flowers, supported on its colder side by the tendrils of ivy, almost of its own age, but on its warmer side maturing a fruitful vine, emblem of the mother and child which gather at the gate, and of the brood of fowls which busily search the wayside.

46. IN WORMLEY WOOD

From the Water-colour in the possession of Mrs. Le Poer Trench.

Painted 1886.

Half a century ago most of the old dwellings on the Surrey border were thatched with good wheaten straw from the Weald of Sussex, but thatch will soon be a thing of the past, partly for the reason that there are no thatchers (or "thackers" as they are called in local midland dialect) left, principally because the straw, of which they consumed a good deal, and which used to be a cheap commodity and not very realisable, in villages whose access to market was difficult, now finds a ready sale.   Locomotion has also enabled slates to be conveyed from hundreds of miles away, and placed on the ground at a less rate than straw.

50. VALEWOOD FARM

51. AN OLD HOUSE AT WEST TARRING

52. AN OLD BUCKINGHAMSHIRE HOUSE

53. DUKE'S COTTAGE

54. THE CONDEMNED COTTAGE

55. ON IDE HILL

56. A CHESHIRE COTTAGE, ALDERLEY EDGE

57. THE SIX BELLS

58. A KENTISH FARMYARD

59. STUDY OF A ROSE BUSH

60. WALLFLOWERS

61. MINNA

62. A KENTISH GARDEN

63. CUTTING CABBAGES

64. IN A SUMMER GARDEN

65. BY THE TERRACE, BROCKET HALL

Thus the old order changeth, and without any regard to the comfort of the tenant, whose roof, as I have already said, instead of consisting of a covering which was warm in winter and cool in summer, is now one which is practically the reverse. Strawen roofs are easy of repair or renewal, and look very trim and cosy when kept in condition.

At the time when this drawing was painted this cottage, lying snugly in the recesses of Wormley Wood (whose pines always attract the attention as the train passes them just before Witley station is reached), was the last specimen of thatch in the neighbourhood, and it only continued so to be through the intervention of a well-known artist who lived not far off. That artist is dead, and probably in the score of years which have since elapsed the thatch has gone the way of the rest, and the harmony of yellowish greys which existed between it and its background have given way to a gaudy contrast of unweathered red tiles or cold unsympathetic blue slates.

The cottage itself may well date back to Tudor times, and the sweetwilliams, pansies, and lavender which border the path leading to it may be the descendants of far-away progenitors, culled by a long-forgotten labourer in his master's "nosegay garden," which at that time was a luxury of the well-to-do only.

Many of the flowers found in this plot of ground were in early days conserved in the gardens of the simple folk rather for their medicinal use than their decorative qualities. Such was certainly the case with lavender. "The floures of lavender do cure the beating of the harte," says one contemporary herbal; and another written in Commonwealth times says, "They are very pleasing and delightful to the brain, which is much refreshed with their sweetness." It was always found in the garden of women who pretended to good housewifery, not only because the heads of the flowers were used for "nosegays and posies," but for putting into "linen and apparel."

47. THE ELDER BUSH, BROOK LANE, WITLEY

From the Water-colour in the possession of Mr. Marcus Huish.

Painted 1887.

Those who are ingenious enough to see the inspiration of another hand in every work that an artist produces would probably raise an outcry against anybody infringing the copyright which they consider that Collins secured more than half a century ago for the children swinging on a gate in his " Happy as a King." But who that examines with any interest or care the figures in this water-colour could for a moment believe that Mrs. Allingham had ever had Collins even unconsciously in her mind when she put in these happy little mortals as adjuncts to her landscape. Having enjoyed at ages such as theirs a swing on many a gate, one can testify that these children must have been seen, studied, and put in from the life and on the spot. See how the elder girl leans over the gate, with perfect self-assurance, directing the boy as to how far back the gate may go; how the younger one has to climb a rung higher than her sister in order to obtain the necessary purchase with her arms, and even then she can only do so with a strain and with a certain nervousness as to the result of the jar when the gate reaches the post on its return. Again, some one has to do the swinging, and Mrs. Allingham has given the proper touch of gallantry by making the second in age of the party, a boy, the first to undertake this part of the business. The excitement of the moment has com-municated itself to the youngest of the family, who raises his stick to cheer as the gate swings to.

Although painted within thirty miles of London, the age of cheap rickety perambulators had not reached the countryside when this drawing was made nearly twenty years ago, and so we see the youngest in a sturdy, hand-made go-cart.

The country folk who passed the artist when she was making this drawing wondered doubtless at her selection of a point of sight where practically nothing but roof and wall of the building were visible, when a few steps farther on its front door and windows might have made a picture ; but the charm of the drawing exists in this simplicity of subject, the greatest pleasure being procurable from the least important features, such, for instance, as the lichen-covered and leek-topped wall, and the untended, buttercup - flecked bank on which it stands.   The locality of the drawing is Brook Lane, near Witley, and the drawing was an almost exact portrait of the cottage as it stood in 1886, but since then it has been modernised like the majority of its fellows, and though the oak-timbered walls, tiled roof, and massive chimney still stand, the old curves of the roof-tree have gone, and American windows have replaced the old lattices.   The other side of the house, as it then appeared, has been preserved to us in the next picture.

48. THE BASKET WOMAN

From the Water-colour in the possession of Mrs. Backhouse.

Painted 1887.

The art critic of *The Times*, in speaking of the Exhibition where this drawing was exhibited, singled it out as " taking rank amongst the very best of Mrs. Allingham's work, and the very model of what an English water-colour should be, with its woodside cottage, its tangled hedges, its background of sombre fir trees, and figures of the girl with basket, and of the cottagers to whom she is offering her wares, showing as it does intense love for our beautiful south country landscape, with the power of seizing its most picturesque aspects with truth of eye and delicacy of hand."

To my mind the most remarkable feature of the drawing is the way in which the long stretch of hedge has been managed.   In most hands it would either be a monotonous and uninteresting feature or an absolute failure, for the difficulty of lending variety of surface and texture to so large a mass is only known to those who have attempted it ; it could only be effected by painting it entirely from nature and on the spot, as was the case here.

Many would have been tempted to break it up by
varieties of garden blooms, but Mrs. Allingham has
only relieved it by a stray spray or two of wild
honeysuckle, which never flowers in masses, and
a few white convolvuli.

That we are not far removed from the small
hop district which is to be found west and northward of this part is evidenced by the hops which
the old woman was in course of plucking from the
pole when her attention was arrested by the
wandering pedlar. This and the apples ripening
on the straggling apple tree show the season to be
early autumn, whereas the elder bush in the
companion drawing puts its season as June.

49. COTTAGE AT SHOTTERMILL, NEAR HASLEMERE

From the Water-colour in the possession of Mr. W. D. Houghton.

Painted 1891.

Each of three counties may practically claim
this cottage for one of its types, for it lies absolutely
at the junction of Surrey, Sussex, and Hampshire.

For a single tenement it is particularly roomy,

and a comfortable one to boot, for its screen of tiles is carried so low down.

It was a curious mood of the artist's to sit down square in front of it and paint its paling paralleling across the picture, a somewhat daring stroke of composition to carry on the line of white tiling with one of white clothes. The sky displays an unusual departure from the artist's custom, as the whole length of it is banked up with banks of cumuli.

The figures and the empty basket point to a little domestic episode. Boy and girl have been sent on an errand, but have not got beyond the farther side of the gate before they betake them-selves to a loll on the grass, which has lengthened out to such an extent that the old grand-dame comes to the cottage door to look for their return, little witting that they are quietly crouched within a few feet of her, hidden behind the paling, over which lavender, sweet-pea, roses, peonies, and hollyhocks nod at them. They are even less conscious of wrong-doing and of impending scold-ings than the cat, which sneaks homewards after a lengthened absence on a poaching expedition.

50. VALEWOOD FARM

From the Water-colour in the possession of the Artist.

Painted 1903.

Valewood is over the ridge which protects Haslemere on the south, and is a very pretty vale of sloping meadows fringed with wood, all under the shadow of Blackdown, to which it belongs. This is distinguished from most houses hereabouts in boasting a stream, the headwater of a string of ponds, whence starts the river Wey northwards on its tortuous journey round the western slopes of Hindhead. When Mrs. Allingham painted the house, which was inhabited by well-to-do yeomen from Devonshire, the dairying and the milking were still conducted by desirable hands, namely, those of milkmaids.

51. AN OLD HOUSE AT WEST TARRING

From the Water-colour in the possession of the Artist.

Painted 1900.

Worthing has been termed "a dull and dreary place, the only relief to which is its suburb of West Tarring." This happening to have been one of the "peculiars" of the Archbishops of Canterbury, has buildings and objects of considerable antiquarian interest.   The cottages which Mrs. Allingham selected for her drawing may be classed amongst them, for they are a type, as good as any in this volume, of the well-built, substantial dwelling-house of our progenitors of many centuries ago—one in which all the features that we have pointed out are to be found.   The house has in course of time clearly become too big for its situation, and has consequently been parcelled out into cottages; this has necessitated some alteration of the front of the lower story, but otherwise it is an exceptionally well-preserved specimen.   Long may it remain so.

52. AN OLD BUCKINGHAMSHIRE HOUSE

From the Water-colour in the possession of Mr. H. W. Birks.

Painted 1899.

This is a somewhat rare instance of the artist selecting for portraiture a house of larger dimensions than a cottage.   It is a singular trait, perhaps a womanly trait, that we never find her choice falling upon the country gentleman's seat, although their formal gardening and parterres of flowers must oftentimes have tempted her.   Her selection, in fact, never rises beyond the wayside tenement, which in that before us no doubt once housed a well-to-do yeoman, but was, when Mrs. Allingham limned it, only tenanted in part by a small farmer and in part by a butcher.   But it is planned and fashioned on the old English lines to which we have referred, and which in the days when it was built governed those of the dwelling of every well-to-do person.

53. DUKE'S COTTAGE

From the Water-colour in the possession of Mr. Maurice Hill.

Painted 1896.

The trend of the trees indicates that this scene is laid where the winds are not only strong, but blow most frequently from one particular quarter. It is, in fact, on the coast of Dorset, at Burton, a little seaside resort of the inhabitants of Bridport, when they want a change from their own water-side town.   The English Channel comes up to one side of the buttercup-clad field, and was behind the artist as she sat to paint the carrier's cottage, a man of some local celebrity, who took the artist to task for not painting his home from a particular point of view, saying, " I've had it painted many a time, and theyse always took it from there." He was a man accustomed to boss the village in a kindly but firm way, never allowing any controversy concerning his charges, which were, however, always reasonable. Hence he had come to be nicknamed " The Duke," and as such did not understand Mrs. Allingham's declining at once to recommence her sketch at the spot he indicated.

The Dorsetshire cottages, for the most part, differ altogether from their fellows in Surrey and Sussex, for their walls are made of what would seem to be the flimsiest and clumsiest materials,—dried mud, intermixed with straw to give it consistency, entering mainly into their composition. Many are not far removed from the Irish cabins, of which we see an example in Plate 78.

54. THE CONDEMNED COTTAGE

From the Water-colour in the possession of the Artist.

Painted 1902.

In speaking of Duke's Cottage, I dwelt upon the poor materials of which it and its Dorsetshire fellows were made, and this, coupled with

Mrs. Allingham presenting a picture of one that is too decayed to live in, may raise a suggestion as to their instability.   But such is not the case.   The lack of substance in the material is made up by increased thickness, and the cottage before us has stood the wear and tear of several hundred years, and now only lacks a tenant through its insanitary condition.   A robin greeted the artist from the topmost of the grass-grown steps, glad no doubt to see some one about the place once more.

55. ON IDE HILL

From the Drawing in the possession of Mr. E. W. Fordham.

Painted 1900.

Ide Hill is to be found in Kent, on the south side of the Westerham Valley, and the old cottage is the last survival of a type, every one of which has given place to the newly built and commonplace.[1] The view from hereabouts is very fine—so fine, indeed, that Miss Octavia Hill has, for some time, been endeavouring, and at last with success, to

[1] Rightly perhaps, for the local doctor pleasantly inquired while she was painting it, why she had selected a house that had had more fever in it than any other in the parish.

preserve a point for the use of the public whence the best can be seen.

56. A CHESHIRE COTTAGE, ALDERLEY EDGE

From the Water-colour in the possession of Mr. A. S. Littlejohns.

Painted 1898.

The almost invariable rule of the south, that cottages are formed out of the local material that is nearest to hand, is clearly not practised farther north, to judge by this example of a typical Cheshire cottage.

Stone is apparently so ready to hand that not only is the roadway paved with it, but even the approach to the cottage, whilst the large blocks seen elsewhere in the picture show that it is not limited in size. Yet the only portion of the building that is constructed of stone, so far as we can see, is the lean-to shed.

The cottage itself differs in many respects from those we have been used to in Surrey and Sussex. The roof is utilised, in fact the level of the first floor is on a line almost with its eaves, and a large bay window in the centre, and one at the end, show that it is well lighted. Heavy barge-boards are affixed to the gables, which is by no means always the case down south, and the wooden frame-work has at one time been blackened in consonance with a custom prevalent in Cheshire and Lanca-shire, but which is probably only of comparatively recent date; for gas-tar, which is used, was not invented a hundred years ago, and there seems no sense in a preservative for oak beams which usually are almost too hard to drive a nail into. The fashion is probably due to the substitution of un-seasoned timber for oak.

57. THE SIX BELLS

From the Water-colour in the possession of Mr. G. Wills.

Painted 1892.

This beautiful old specimen of a timbered house was discovered by Mrs. Allingham by accident when staying with some artistic friends at Bearsted, in Kent, who were unaware of its existence. Although the weather was very cold and the season late, she lost no time in painting it, as its inmates said that it would be pulled down directly its owner, an old lady of ninety-two, who was very ill, died. Having spent a long day absorbed in putting down on paper its intricate details, she went into the house for a little warmth and a cup of tea, only to find a single fire, by which sat a labourer with his pot of warmed ale on the hob. Asking whether she could not go to some other fire, she was assured that nowhere else in the house could one be lit, as water lay below all the floors, and a fire caused this to evaporate and fill the rooms with steam.

As we have said, Mrs. Allingham alters her compositions as little as possible when painting from Nature, but in this case she has omitted a church tower that stood just to the right of the inn, and added the tall trees behind it. The omission was due to a feeling that the house itself was the point, and a quite sufficient point of interest, that would only be lessened by a competing one. The addition of the trees was made in order to give value to the grey of the house-side, which would have been considerably diminished by a broad expanse of sky.

58. A KENTISH FARMYARD

From the Water-colour in the possession of Mr. Arthur R. Moro.

Painted 1900.

Farmyards are out of fashion nowadays, and a Royal Water-Colour Society's Exhibition, which in

the days of Prout and William Hunt probably contained a dozen of them, will now find place for a
single example only from the hand of Mr. Wilmot
Pilsbury, who alone faithfully records for us the
range of straw-thatched buildings sheltering an
array of picturesque waggons and obsolete farming
implements.   But this "stead" is just opposite to
the farm in which Mrs. Allingham stays, and it
has often attracted her on damp days by its looking like "a blaze of raw sienna."   We can understand the tiled expanse of steep-pitched, moss-
covered roof affording her some of that material
on which her heart delights, and which she has
felt it a duty to hand down to posterity before it
gives place to some corrugated iron structure which
must, ere long, supplant this old timber-built barn.

What was originally a study has been trans-
formed by her, through the human incidents, into
a picture : the milkmaid carrying the laden pail
from the byre ; the cock on the dunghill, seemingly
amazed that his wives are too busily engaged on
its contents to admire him ; the lily-white ducks
waddling to the pool to indulge in a drink, the
gusto of which seems to increase in proportion to
the questionableness of its quality.

CHAPTER VIII

GARDENS AND ORCHARDS

One is nearer God's heart in a garden
Than anywhere else on earth.

THE practice of painting gardens is almost as modern as that of painting by ladies. The Flemings of the fifteenth century, it is true, introduced in a delightful fashion conventional borders of flowers into some of their pictures, probably because they felt that ornament must be presented from end to end of them, and that in no way could they do this better than by adding the gaiety of flowers to their foregrounds. But all through the later dreary days no one touched the garden, for the conglomeration of flowers in the pieces of the Dutchmen of the seventeenth century cannot be treated as such. Flowers certainly flourished in the gardens of the well-to-do in England in the century between 1750 and 1850,

but none of the limners of the drawings of noble-
men or of gentlemen's seats which were produced
in such quantities during that period ever con-
descended to introduce them. Even so late as
fifty years ago, if we may judge from the titles,
the Royal Academy Exhibition of that date did
not contain a single specimen of a flower-garden.
The only probable one is a picture entitled " Cottage Roses," and any remotely connected with the
garden appear under such headings as " Early
Tulips," " Geraniums," " Japonicas and Orchids,"
" Will you have this pretty rose, Mamma?" or
" The Last Currants of Summer"! Taste only
half a century ago was different from ours, and
asked for other provender. Thus, the original
owner of the catalogue from which these statistics
were taken was an energetic amateur critic, who
has commended, or otherwise, almost every picture,
commendations being signified by crosses and disapproval by noughts. The only work with five
crosses is one illustrating the line, " Now stood
Eliza on the wood-crown'd height." On the other
hand, Millais' " Peace Concluded" stands at the
head of the bad marks with five, his " Blind Girl"
with two, which number is shared with Leighton's
" Triumph of Music." Holman Hunt's " Scape-

goat," in addition to four bad marks, is described as "detestable and profane." These pre-Raphaelites, Millais, Holman Hunt, and their followers, then so little esteemed, may in truth be said to have been the originators of the "garden-drawing cult," chief amongst their followers being Frederick Walker. To the example of the last-named more especially are due the productions of the numerous artists—good, bad, and indifferent—who have seized upon a delightful subject and almost nauseated the public with their productions. The omission of gardens from the painter's *rôle* in later times may in a measure have been due to the gardens themselves, or, to speak more correctly, to those under whose charge they were maintained. The ideal of a garden to the true artist must always have differed from these as to its ordering, even in these very recent days when the edict has gone forth that Nature is to be allowed a hand in the planning

The gardener, no matter whether the surroundings favour a formal garden or not, insists upon his harmonies or contrasts of brilliant colourings. If he takes these from a manual on gardening he will adopt what is termed a procession of colouring somewhat as follows: strong blues, pale yellow, pink, crimson, strong scarlet, orange, and bright yellow. He is told that his colours are to be placed with careful deliberation and forethought, as a painter employs them in his picture, and not dropped down as he has them on his palette! Alfred Parsons and George Elgood have on occasions grappled with creations such as these, when placed in settings of yew-trimmed hedges, or as surroundings of a central statue, or sundial; but who will say that the results have been as successful as those where formality has been merely a suggestion, and Nature has had her say and her way. Surroundings must, of course, play a prominent part in any garden scheme. However much we may dislike a stiff formality, it is sometimes a necessity. For instance, herbaceous plants, with annuals of mixed colours, would have looked out of place on the lawn in front of Brocket Hall (Plate 65), which calls for a mass of plants of uniform colours. The lie of the ground, too, must, as in such a case, be taken into account: there it is a sloping descent facing towards the sun, and so is not easy to keep in a moist condition. Geraniums and calceolarias, which stand such conditions, are therefore almost a necessity.

When this book was proposed to Mrs. Allingham her chief objection was her certainty that no process could reproduce her drawings satisfactorily. Her method of work was, she believed, entirely opposed to mechanical reproduction, for she employed not only every formula used by her fellow water-colourists, but many that others would not venture upon. Amongst those she tabulated was her system of obtaining effects by rubbing, scrubbing, and scratching. But the process was not to be denied, and she was fain to admit that even in these it has been a wonderfully faithful reproducer. Now nowhere are these methods of Mrs. Allingham's more utilised, and with greater effect, than in her drawings of flower-gardens. The system of painting flowers in masses has undergone great changes of late. The plan adopted a generation or so ago was first to draw and paint the flowers and then the foliage. This method left the flowers isolated objects and the foliage without substantiality. Mrs. Allingham's method is the reverse of this. Take, for instance, the white clove pinks in the foreground of Mrs. Combe's drawing of the kitchen-garden at Farringford (Plate 71). These are so admirably done that their perfume almost scents the room. They have been simply carved out of a background of walk and grey-green spikes, and left as white paper, all their drawing and modelling being achieved by a dexterous use of the knife and a wetted and rubbed surface. The poppies, roses, columbines, and stocks have all been created in the same way. The advantage is seen at once. There are no badly pencilled outlines, and the blooms blend amongst themselves and grow naturally out of their foliage.

---

59. STUDY OF A ROSE BUSH

From the Water-colour in the possession of the Artist.

Painted about 1887.

A very interesting series of studies of various kinds might have been included in this volume, which would have shown the thoroughness with which our artist works, and it was with much reluctance that we discarded all but two, in the interests of the larger number of our readers, who might have thought them better fitted for a manual of instruction. The Gloire de Dijon rose, however, is such a prime old favourite, begotten before the days of scentless specimens to which are appended the ill-sounding names of fashionable patrons of the rose-grower, that we could not keep our hands off it when we came across it in the artist's portfolio.

This rose tree, or one of its fellows, will be seen in the background of two of the drawings of Mrs. Allingham's garden at Sandhills, namely, Plate 61 (*Frontispiece*) and Plate 64.

60. WALLFLOWERS

From the Water-colour in the possession of Mr. F. G. Debenham.

Painted about 1893.

Of the denizens of the garden there is perhaps none which appeals to a countryman who has drifted into the city so much as the wallflower. His senses both of sight and smell have probably grown up under its influence, and it carries him back to the home of his childhood, for it is of never-to-be-forgotten sweetness both in colour and in scent, and it conjures up old days when the rare warmth of an April sun extracted its perfume until all the air in its neighbourhood was redolent of it.

If my reader be a west countryman, like the author, he may best know it as the gilliflower, but he will do so erroneously, for the name rightly applies to the carnation, and was so used even in Chaucer's time—

Many a clove gilofre
To put in ale ;

and again in Culpepper—

The great clove carnation Gillo-Floure.

But as a "rose by any other name would smell as sweet," every true flower-lover cherishes his wall-flower, which returns to him so bountifully the slightest attention, which accepts the humblest position, which thrives on the scantiest fare, which is amongst the first to welcome us in the spring, and, with its scantier second bloom, amongst the last to bid adieu in the autumn, sometimes even striving to gladden us with its blossom year in and year out if winter's cold be not too stark.

Old names give place to new, and in nursery-men's catalogues we search in vain for its pleasant-sounding title, and fail to distinguish either its reproduction in black and white, or its designation under that of cheiranthus.

61. MINNA

From the Water-colour in the possession of the Lord Chief Justice of England.

Painted about 1886.

This, and the drawing of a "Summer Garden" (Plate 64), are taken almost from the same spot in

Mrs. Allingham's garden at Sandhills.   Both are
simple studies of flowers without any more
elaborate effort at arrangement or composition
than that which gives to each a purposed scheme
of colour—a scheme, however, that is, with set
purpose, hidden away, so that the flowers may
look as if they grew, as they appear to do,
by chance.   The flowers, too, are old-fashioned
inhabitants : pansies, sea-pinks, marigolds, sweetwilliams, snap-dragons, eschscholtzias, and flags,
with a background of rose bushes ; all of them
(with the exception, perhaps, of the flag) flowers
such as Spenser might have had in his eye when
he penned the lines—

> No daintie flowre or herbe that growes on grownd,
> No arborett with painted blossomes drest
> And smelling sweete, but there it might be fownd
> To bud out faire, and throwe her sweete smels al arownd.

62. A KENTISH GARDEN

From the Drawing in the possession of the Artist.

Painted 1903.

This scene may well be compared with that of
Tennyson's garden at Aldworth, reproduced in

Plate 74, as it illustrates even more appositely
than does that, the lines in "Roses on the Terrace"
concerning the contrast between the pink of the
flower and the blue of the distance.   But here
the interval between the colours is not the
exaggerated fifty miles of the poem, but one
insufficient to dim the shapes of the trees on the
opposite side of the valley.   Of all the gardens
here illustrated none offers a greater wealth of
colour than this Kentish garden, situated as it is
with an aspect which makes it a veritable sun-trap.

63. CUTTING CABBAGES

From the Water-colour in the possession of Mr. E. W. Fordham.

Painted about 1884.

The cabbage is probably to most people the
most uninteresting tenant of the kitchen-garden,
and yet its presence there was probably the motive
which set Mrs. Allingham to work to make this
drawing, for it is clear that in the first instance it
was conceived as a study of the varied and delicate
mother-of-pearl hues which each presented to an
artistic eye.   As a piece of painting it is extremely
meritorious through its being absolutely straight-

forward drawing and brush work, the high lights
being left, and not obtained by the usual method
of cutting, scraping, or body colour. The buxom
mother of a growing family selecting the best plant
for their dinner is just the personal note which
distinguishes each and every one of our illustrations.

64. IN A SUMMER GARDEN

From the Water-colour in the possession of Mr. William Newall.

Painted about 1887.

I cannot refrain from drawing attention to this
reproduction as one of the wonders of the "three
colour process." If my readers could see the three
colours which produce the result when super-
imposed, first the yellow, then the red, and lastly
the blue—aniline hues of the most forbidding
character—they would indeed deem it incredible
that any resemblance to the original could be
possible. It certainly passes the comprehension
of the uninitiated how the differing delicacies of
the violet hues of the flowers to the left could
be obtained from a partnership which produced
the blue black of the flowers in the foreground,
the light pinks of the Shirley poppies, and the rich

reds of the sweetwilliams.   Again, what a marvel
must the photographic process be which refuses
to recognise the snow - white campanula, and
leaves it to be defined by the untouched paper,
and yet records the faint pink flush which has
been breathed upon the edges of the sweetwilliam.
It is indeed a tribute to the inventive genius of
the present day, genius which will probably enable
the "press the button and we do the rest photo-
grapher" before many days are past to reel off
in colour what he now can only accomplish in
monochrome.

65. BY THE TERRACE, BROCKET HALL

From the Water-colour in the possession of Lord Mount-Stephen.

Painted 1900.

Portraiture of time-worn cottages where Nature
has its way, and cottars' gardens where flowers
come and go at their own sweet will, is a very
different thing from portraiture of a well-kept
house, where the bricklayer and the mason are
requisitioned when the slightest decay shows itself,
and of gardens where formal ribbon borders are
laid out by so-called landscape gardeners, whose

taste always leans to bright colours not always massed in the happiest way. In portraits of houses license is hardly permissible even for artistic effects, for not only may associations be connected with every slope and turn of a path, but the artist always has before him the possibility that the drawing will be hung in close proximity to the scene, for comparison by persons who may not always be charitably disposed to artistic alterations. It speaks well, therefore, for Mrs. Allingham in the drawing of the garden at Brocket that she has produced a drawing which, without offending the conventions, is still a picture harmonious in colour, and probably very satisfying to the owner. There are few who would have cared to essay the very difficult drawing of cedars, and have accomplished it so well, or have laboured with so much care over the plain-faced house and windows. As to these latter she has been happy in assisting the sunlight in the picture by the drawn-down blinds at the angles which the sun reaches. The scene has clearly been pictured in the full blaze of summer.

Brocket Hall is a mansion some three miles north of Hatfield, Hertfordshire, and a short distance off the Great North Road. It is one of a

string of seats hereabouts which belong to Earl
Cowper, but has been tenanted by Lord Mount-
Stephen for some years.   The house, which, as
will be seen, has not much architectural preten-
sions, was built in the eighteenth century, but
it is, to cite an old chronicle, "situate on a
dry hill in a fair park well wooded and greatly
timbered" through which the river Lea winds
picturesquely.   It is notable as having been the
residence of two Prime Ministers, Lord Mel-
bourne and Lord Palmerston.   The drawing of
"The Hawthorn Valley" (Plate 37) is taken from
a part of the park.

66. THE SOUTH BORDER

From the Water-colour in the possession of the Artist.

Painted 1902.

This is one of the borders designed on the
graduated doctrine as practised by Miss Jekyll
in her garden at Munstead near Godalming.
Here we have the colours starting at the far end
in grey leaves, whites, blues, pinks, and pale
yellows, towards a gorgeous centre of reds, oranges,
and scarlets, the whites being formed of yuccas,

the pinks of hollyhocks, the reds and yellows of gladioli, nasturtiums, African marigolds, herbaceous sunflowers, dahlias, and geraniums. Another part of the scheme is seen in the drawing which follows.

67. THE SOUTH BORDER

From the Water-colour in the possession of W. Edwards, Jun.

Painted 1900.

A further illustration of the same border in Miss Jekyll's garden, but painted a year or two earlier, and representing it at its farther end, where cool colours are coming into the scheme. The orange-red flowers hanging over the wall are those of the *Bignonia grandiflora ;* the bushes on either side of the archway with white flowers are choisyas, and the adjoining ones are red and yellow dahlias, flanked by tritonias (red-hot pokers); the oranges in front are African marigolds (hardly reproduced sufficiently brightly), with white marguerites; the grey-leaved plant to the left is the *Cineraria maritima.* Miss Jekyll does not entirely keep to her arrangement of masses of colour ; whilst, as an artist, she affects rich masses of colour, she is not above experimenting by breaking in varieties.

68. STUDY OF LEEKS

From the Water-colour in the possession of the Artist.

Painted 1902.

I like the leeke above all herbes and flowers,
When first we wore the same the field was ours.
The Leeke is White and Greene, whereby is ment
That Britaines are both stout and eminent;
Next to the Lion and the Unicorn,
The Leeke's the fairest emblym that is worne.

When Mrs. Allingham in wandering round a
garden came upon this bed of flowering leeks,
and, "singularly moved to love the lovely that
are not beloved," at once sat down to paint it in
preference to a more ambitious display in the
front garden that was at her service, her friends
probably considered her artistic perception to be
peculiar, and some there may be who will deem
the honour given to it by introduction into these
pages to be more than its worth.   But it has
more than one claim to recognition here, for it is
unusual in subject, delicate in its violet tints, not
unbecoming in form, and is here disassociated
from the disagreeable odour which usually accom-
panies the reality.

66. THE SOUTH BORDER

67. THE SOUTH BORDER

68. STUDY OF LEEKS

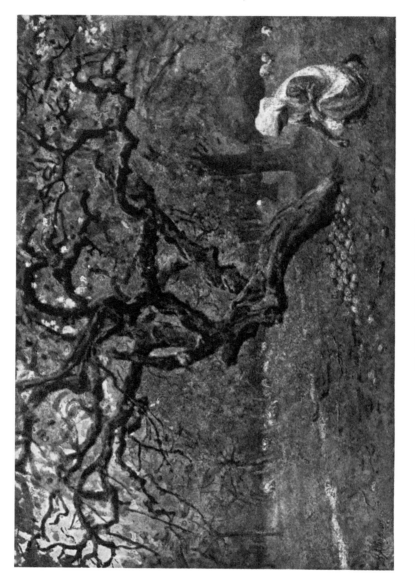

69. THE APPLE ORCHARD

70. THE HOUSE, FARRINGFORD

71. THE KITCHEN-GARDEN, FARRINGFORD

72. THE DAIRY, FARRINGFORD

73. ONE OF LORD TENNYSON'S COTTAGES.

FARRINGFORD

74. A GARDEN IN OCTOBER, ALDWORTH

75. HOOK HILL FARM, FRESHWATER

76. AT POUND GREEN, FRESHWATER, ISLE OF WIGHT

77. A COTTAGE AT FRESHWATER GATE

78. A CABIN AT BALLYSHANNON

79. THE FAIRY BRIDGES

80. THE CHURCH OF STA. MARIA DELLA

SALUTE, VENICE

81. A FRUIT STALL, VENICE

69. THE APPLE ORCHARD

From the Water-colour in the possession of Mrs. Dobson.

Painted about 1877.

Originally, no doubt, a study of one of those subjects which artists like to attack, a misshapen tree presenting every imaginable contortion of foreshortened curvature to harass and worry the draughtsman,—a tree, specimens of which are too often to be found in old orchards of this size, whose bearing time has long departed, and who now only cumber the ground, and with their many fellows have had much to do with the gradual decay of the English apple industry.

CHAPTER IX

TENNYSON'S HOMES

FEW poets have been so fortunate in their residences
as was the great Poet Laureate of the Victorian
era in the two which he for many years called his
own.   Selected in the first instance for their beauty
and their seclusion, they had other advantages
which fitted them admirably to a poet's temperament.

Farringford, at the western end of the Isle of
Wight, was the first to be acquired, being purchased
in 1853; it was Tennyson's home for forty years,
and the house wherein most of his best-known
works were written.   At the time when it came
into his hands communication with the mainland
was of the most primitive description, and the poet
and his wife had to cross the Solent in a rowing-
boat.   So far removed was he from intrusion
there that he could indulge in what to him were

favourite pastimes—sweeping up the leaves, mow-
ing the grass, gravelling the walks, and digging the
beds—without interruption. Many of the visitors
which railway and steamship facilities brought to
the neighbourhood in later years felt that he set the
boundary within which no foot other than his own
and that of his friends should tread at an extreme
limit. Golfers over the Needles Links—persons
who, perhaps, are prone to consider that whatever
is capable of being made into a course should be
so utilised—were wont to look with covetous eyes
over a portion of the downs that would have
formed a much-needed addition to their course,
but over which no ball was allowed to be played.
But the pertinacity of the crowd, in endeavouring
to get a sight of the Laureate, necessitated an
inexorable rule if the retreat was to be what it
was intended, namely, a place for work and for
rest.

Mrs. Tennyson thus described "her wild house
amongst the pine trees" :—

The golden green of the trees, the burning splendour of
Blackgang Chine, and the red bank of the primeval river
contrasted with the turkis blue of the sea (that is our view
from the drawing-room) make altogether a miracle of beauty
at sunset. We are glad that Farringford is ours.

Although at times the weather can be cold and bleak enough in this sheltered corner of the Isle of Wight, and

> The scream of a madden'd beach
> Dragged down by the wave

must oftentimes have "shocked the ear" in the Farringford house, the climate is too relaxing an one for continued residence, and Tennyson's second house, Aldworth, was well chosen as a contrast. Aubrey Vere thus describes it :—

It lifted England's great poet to a height from which he could gaze on a large portion of that English land which he loved so well, see it basking in its most affluent beauty, and only bound by the inviolate sea.

The house stands at an elevation of some six hundred feet above the sea, on the spur of Blackdown, which is the highest ground in Sussex, on a steep side towards the Weald, just where the greensand hills break off. It is some two miles from Haslemere, and just within the Sussex border.

Two of the drawings connected with these houses, which are reproduced here, were painted before Tennyson's death, namely, in 1890.

The house at Farringford was drawn in the spring, when the lawn was pied with daisies, and

the Laureate required his heavy cloak to guard him
from the keenness of the April winds.

The kitchen-garden at Farringford, which somewhat belies its name, for flowers encroach everywhere upon the vegetables, and the apple trees rise
amidst a parterre of blossom, was painted in its
summer aspect, when it was gay with pinks, stocks,
rockets, larkspurs, delphiniums, aubrietias, eschscholtzias, and big Oriental poppies. Tennyson
visited it almost daily to take the record of the rain-
gauge and thermometer, which can be descried in
the drawing about half-way down the path.

The kitchen-garden at Aldworth opens up a
very different prospect to the banked-up background of trees at Farringford. Standing at a very
considerable elevation, it commands a magnificent
view over the Weald of Sussex. The spot is referred to in the poem " Roses on the Terrace '
in the volume entitled *Demeter*, thus—

> This red flower, which on our terrace here,
> Glows in the blue of fifty miles away ;

as also in the lines—

> Green Sussex fading into blue,
> With one grey glimpse of sea.

It was this view that the dying poet longed to see

once again on his last morning when he cried, "I want the blinds up! I want to see the sky and the light!"

The time of year when Mrs. Allingham painted it was October, and a wet October too, for two umbrellas even could not keep her from getting wet through.

It is rare for Mrs. Allingham to set her flowers so near the horizon as in this case,—in fact I only remember having seen another instance of it,— but no doubt the same feeling that appealed to the poet's eye, and impelled him to pen the lines we have quoted, fascinated the artist's, namely, the beautiful appearance of the varied hues of flowers against a background of delicate blue.

October is the saddest time of year for the garden, but a basket full of gleanings at that time is more cherished than one in the full heyday of its magnificence. Here the apple tree has already shed most of its leaves, the hollyhock stems are baring, and autumnal flowers, in which yellow so much predominates, as, for instance, the great marigold, the herbaceous sunflower, and the calliopsis, are much in evidence. Nasturtiums and every free-growing creeper have long ere this trailed their stems over the box edging, and made an untidiness which forebodes their early destruction at the hands of the gardener. Of sweet-scented flowers only a few peas and mignonette remain.

Mr. Allingham knew the Poet Laureate for many years, having at one time lived at Lymington, which is the port of departure for the western end of the Isle of Wight, and whence he often crossed to Farringford. The artist's first meeting with Tennyson was soon after her marriage. He and his son Hallam had come up to town, and had walked over from Mr. James Knowles's house at Clapham, where they were staying, to Chelsea. He invited Mrs. Allingham to Aldworth, an invitation which was accepted shortly afterwards. The poet was very proud of the country which framed his house, and during this visit he took her his special walks to Blackdown, to Fir Tree Corner (whence there is a wide view over the Weald towards the sea), and to a great favourite of his, the Foxes' Hole, a lovely valley beyond his own grounds. Whilst on this last-named ramble he suddenly turned round and chided the artist for " chattering instead of looking at the view." During this visit he read to her a part of his *Harold*, and the wonder of his voice and whole manner of reading or chanting she will never forget.

When the Allinghams came to live at Witley they were able to get to and from Aldworth in an afternoon, and so were frequent visitors there. One day in the autumn of 1881 Mrs. Allingham went over alone, owing to her husband's absence, and after lunch the poet walked with her to Foxes' Hole, where they sat on bundles of pea-sticks, she painting an old cottage since pulled down, and he watching her. After a time he said slowly, " I should like to do that. It does not look very difficult." Years later he showed her some water-colour drawings he had made, from imagination, of Mount Ida clad in dark fir groves, which were undoubtedly very clever in their suggestiveness.

Lord Tennyson's Isle of Wight home Mrs. Allingham did not see until after she returned to live in London, when Mr. Hallam Tennyson, in conversing with her about her drawings, told her that if she would come to the Isle of Wight he could show her some fine old cottages. She accordingly went at the Easter of 1890 to Fresh-water, when he was as good as his word, and she at once began drawings of " The Dairy " and

the cottage "At Pound Green." Miss Kate
Greenaway, who had come to stay with her,
also painted them. The next spring, and many
springs afterwards, Mrs. Allingham went to Freshwater, generally after the Easter holidays.

During one of these stays she accompanied
Birket Foster to Farringford, and the poet asked
the two artists to come for a walk with him.
There happened to be a boy of the party in a
sailor costume with a bright blue collar and a
scarlet cap, and Birket Foster, who was at the
moment walking behind with Mrs. Allingham,
said, "Why is that red and blue so disagreeable?"
Tennyson's quick ear caught something, and he
turned on them, setting his stick firmly in the
ground, and asked Mr. Foster to explain himself.
"Well," Mr. Foster said, "I only know that the
effect of the contrast is to make cold water run
down my spine." Mrs. Allingham cordially agreed
with Mr. Birket Foster, but Tennyson could not
feel the "cold water," although he saw their point,
and said it was doubtless with painters as with
himself in poetry, namely, that some combinations
of sound gave intense pleasure, whilst others
grated, and he quoted certain lines as being so to
him. On another occasion, whilst walking with

him at Freshwater, he said something which led Mrs. Allingham to mention that she generally kept her drawings by her for a long time, often for years, working on them now and again and considering about figures and incidents for them,[1] upon which he remarked that it was the same in the case of poems, and that he used generally to keep his by him, often in print, for a considerable time before publishing.

THE following drawings have been sufficiently described in the text :—

70. THE HOUSE, FARRINGFORD

From the Water-colour in the possession of Mr. John Mackinnon.

Painted 1890.

71. THE KITCHEN-GARDEN, FARRINGFORD

From the Water-colour in the possession of Mrs. Combe.

Painted 1894.

72. THE DAIRY, FARRINGFORD

From the Water-colour in the possession of Mr. Douglas Freshfield.

Painted 1890.

---

[1] Mrs. Allingham's friends sometimes say to her, "You paint so quickly." Her reply is, "Perhaps I make a quick beginning, but I take a long time to finish." Which is the fact.

73. ONE OF LORD TENNYSON'S COTTAGES, FARRINGFORD

From the Water-colour in the possession of Mr. E. Marsh Simpson.

Painted 1900.

74. A GARDEN IN OCTOBER, ALDWORTH

From the Water-colour in the possession of Mr. F. Pennington.

Painted 1891.

The next three water-colours find a place here, as having been painted during visits to the Island.

75. HOOK HILL FARM, FRESHWATER

From the Water-colour in the possession of Sir James Kitson, Bt., M.P.

Painted 1891.

An old farmhouse on the other side of the Yar Valley to Farringford, but one which Tennyson often made an object for a walk. It possessed a fine yard and old thatch-covered barn, which, however, has passed out of existence, but not before Mrs. Allingham had perpetuated it in water-colour. This group of buildings has been painted by the artist from every side, and at other seasons than that represented here, when pear, apple, and lilac trees, primroses, and daisies

vie with one another in heralding the coming
spring.

76. AT POUND GREEN, FRESHWATER, ISLE OF WIGHT

From the Water-colour in the possession of Mr. Douglas Freshfield.

Painted about 1891.

To the cottage-born child of to-day the name
of the "Pound" has little significance, but even
in the writer's recollection it not only had a
fascination but a feeling almost akin to terror,
being deemed, in very truth, to be a prison for
the dumb animals who generally, through no fault
of their own, were impounded there.   Both it and
its tenants too were always suggestive of starva-
tion.   When (following, at some interval of time,
the village stocks) it passed out of use, the countryside, in losing both, forgot a very cruel phase of
life.

A child of to-day has, with all its education,
not acquired many amusements to replace that
of teasing the tenants of the Pound on the Green,
so he never tires of pulling anything with the
faintest similitude to the cart which he will probably spend much of his later life in driving.   Here

the youngster has evidently been making stabling for his toy under a seat whose back is formed out of some carved relic of an old sailing-ship that was probably wrecked at the Needles, and whose remains the tide carried in to Freshwater Bay.

77. A COTTAGE AT FRESHWATER GATE

From the Water-colour in the possession of Sir Henry Irving.

Painted 1891.

Tramps are usually few and far between in the Isle of Wight, for the reason that the island does not rear many, and those from the mainland do not care to cross the Solent lest, should they be tempted to wrong-doing, there may be a difficulty in avoiding the arm of the law or the confines of the island. It is somewhat surprising, therefore, to find the only flaw in our title of *Happy England* in such a locality. But here it is, on this spring day, when apple, and pear, and primrose blossoms make one

Bless His name
That He hath mantled the green earth with flowers.

We have the rift, making the discordant note, of want, in the person of a woman, dragged down with the burden of four children, sending the

eldest to beg a crust at a house which cannot
contain a superfluity of the good things of this
world.

A singular interest attaches to Mrs. Allingham's drawing of this cottage.   She had nearly
completed it on a Saturday afternoon, and was
asked by a friend whether she would finish it next
day.   To this she replied that she never sketched
in public on Sunday.   On Monday the cottage
was a heap of ruins, having been burnt down the
previous night.

CHAPTER X

THAT a true artist is always individual, and that his work is always affected by some one or other of his predecessors or contemporaries, would appear to be a paradox : nevertheless it is a proposition that few will dispute. Art has been practised for too long a period, and by too many talented professors, for entirely novel views or treatments of Nature to be possible, and whilst an artist may be entirely unaware that he has imbibed anything from others, it is certain that if he has had eyes to see he must have done so.

I have already stated that Mrs. Allingham's work, whether in subject or execution, is, so far as she is aware, entirely her own, and it would, perhaps, be quite sufficient were I to leave the matter after having placed that assertion on record. To go farther may perhaps lay oneself open to the

charge, *qui s'excuse s'accuse.*   I trust not, and that
I may be deemed to be only doing my duty if I
deal at some length with comparisons that have
been made between her work and that of certain
other artists.

The two names with whose productions those
of Mrs. Allingham are most frequently linked are
Frederick Walker and Birket Foster : the first in
connection with her figures, the latter with her
cottage subjects.

As regards these two artists it must be remembered that both their and her early employment lay in the same direction, namely, that of
book illustration, and therefore each started with
somewhat similar methods of execution and subject,
varied only by leanings towards the style of any
work they came in contact with, or by their own
individuality.

That both had much in common is well known ;
in fact, Mrs. Allingham used to tell Mr. Foster
that she considered him, as did others, the father
of Walker and Pinwell.

In the case of Frederick Walker, his career
was at its most interesting phase whilst Mrs.
Allingham was a student.   Her first visit to the
Royal Academy was probably in 1868, when his

" Vagrants " was exhibited, to be followed in 1869 by " The Old Gate," in 1870 by " The Plough," and in 1872 by " The Harbour of Refuge."

It must not be forgotten that the name of Frederick Walker was at this time in every one's mouth, that is, every one who could be deemed to be included in the small Art world of those days. The painter visitors to the Academy schools sang his praises to the students, and he himself fascinated and charmed them with his boyish and graceful presence. As Mrs. Allingham says, everybody in the schools " adored " him and his work, and on the opening of the Academy doors on the first Monday in May the students rushed to his picture first of all.

To contradict a dictum of Walker's in those days was the rankest heresy in a student. Mrs. Allingham remembers an occasion when a painter was holding forth on the right methods of water-colour work, asserting that the paper should be put flat down on a table, as was the custom with the old men, and the colour should be laid on in washes and left to dry with edges, and if Walker taught any other method he was wrong. Mrs. Allingham and her fellow-students were furious at their hero being possibly in fault, and asked for the opinion of an Academician.   His reply was : " And *who* is Mr. ——, and how does *he* paint that *he* should lay down the law ?   If Walker *is* all wrong with his methods, he paints like an angel."

Mrs. Allingham's confession of faith is this : " I *was* influenced, doubtless, by his work.   I adored it, but I never consciously copied it.   It revealed to me certain beauties and aspects of Nature, as du Maurier's had done, and as North's and others have since done, and then I saw like things for myself in Nature, and painted them, I truly think, in my own way—not the best way, I dare say, but in the only way *I* could."

Those, therefore, who discover not the reflection but the inspiration of Walker in the idyllic grace of Mrs. Allingham's figures, and in her treatment of flowers, place her in a company which she readily accepts, and is proud of.

But it is with Birket Foster that our artist's name has been more intimately linked by the critics, some even going to the length of asserting that without him there would have been no Mrs. Allingham.

Having had the pleasure of an intimacy with Birket Foster, which extended to writing his biography (*Birket Foster : His Life and Work,*

Virtue and Co., 1890), I can emphatically assert that he never held that opinion, but stated that she had struck out a line which was entirely her own, and, as he generously added, "with much more modernity in it than mine."

There are, however, so many similarities between their artistic careers that I may be excused for dwelling on some of them, for they no doubt unconsciously influenced not only the method of their work but the subject of it.

Drawing in black and white on wood in each case formed the groundwork of their education, and was only followed by colour at a subsequent stage.

Both, having determined to support themselves, were fain to seek out the engravers and obtain from them a livelihood. Birket Foster at sixteen was fortunate enough to meet in Landells one who at once recognised his capabilities, whilst Mrs. Allingham found a similar friend in Joseph Swain. Again, book illustration was as much in vogue in 1870 as it was in 1842; and by another coincidence both years witnessed the birth of an illustrated weekly, for Birket Foster, in 1842, was employed upon the infant *Illustrated London News*, while Mrs. Allingham was the only lady to whom Mr. Thomas allotted some of the early work on the

Graphic. Differences there were in their opportunities, and these were not always in the lady's
favour.   Birket Foster found in Landells a man
who looked after his youngster's education, and,
convinced that Nature was his best mistress, sent
him to her with these instructions: "Now that
work is slack in these summer months, spend them
in the fields; take your colours and copy every
detail of the scene as carefully as possible, especially
trees and foreground plants, and come up to me
once a month and show me what you have done."
A splendid memory aided Foster in his studies all
too well, for he learnt to draw with such absolute
fidelity every detail that he required, that he never
again required to go to Nature.   That he did
so we know from his repeated visits to every part
of Europe—visits resulting in delightful work;
but what the world saw was entirely studio work,
and this tended to a repetition which oftentimes
marred the entire satisfaction that one otherwise
derived from his drawings.   Mrs. Allingham herself, although living close to and engaged on the
same subjects, never came across him painting out
of doors, and only once saw him note-book in
hand.

Chance influenced the two careers also in another

way, which might have made any similarity between them altogether out of question. The first commission to illustrate a book which Miss Paterson obtained was a prose work, in which figures and household scenes entirely predominated,—in fact, all her black-and-white work was of this homely nature,—and for some years she had no call for the delineation of landscape. With Foster it was not very different. It is true that his first commission was *The Boys' Spring and Summer Book*, in which he had to draw the seasons, and to draw them afield. But this might not have attracted him to landscape work, for his patron's next commission was quite in another direction. I may be excused for referring to it at length, for the little-known incident is of some interest now that the actors in it have each achieved such world-wide reputations. Certain of the young pre-Raphaelites, including Rossetti, Burne-Jones, and Millais, had been entrusted with the illustration of *Evangeline*. The result was a perfect staggerer to the publisher Bogue, who was altogether unable to appreciate their revolutionary methods. "What shall I do with them?" he was asked by the engraver to whom he showed the blocks on which most elaborate designs had been most lovingly drawn.

"This," said Bogue, and wetting one of them he erased the drawing with the sleeve of his coat, serving each in turn in the same way.

After this drastic treatment the *Evangeline* commission was handed over to Birket Foster. It can be easily imagined with what trepidation he, knowing these facts, approached and carried out his task, and his delight when even the *Athenæum* could say, " A more lovely book than this has rarely been given to the public." The success of the work was enormous. His career was apparently henceforth marked out as an illustrator of verse in black and white, for his popularity continued until it was not a question of giving him commissions, but of what book there was for him to illustrate; and he used laughingly to say that finally there was nothing left for him but Young's *Night Thoughts* and Pollok's *Course of Time.*[1]

Thus we see that Birket Foster's art work was for long confined to subjects as to which he had no

---

[1] When will the day come that editions of the books illustrated by Birket Foster will attain to their proper value? The poets illustrated by miserable process blocks find a sale, whilst these volumes, issued in the middle of the last century, and containing the finest specimens of the wood-cutting art, attract, if we may judge by the second-hand booksellers' catalogues, no purchasers even at a sum which is a fraction of their original price.

voice, but which certainly influenced his art, and it says much for his temperament that throughout it warranted the term "poetical." In like manner it is much to Mrs. Allingham's credit that her prosaic start did not prevent the same quality welling up and being always in evidence in her productions.

If I have not wearied the reader I would like to point out some further coincidences in their careers which are of interest.

Birket Foster became a water-colourist through the chance that he could not sell his oil-paintings, which consequently cumbered his small working-room to such an extent that one night he cut them all from their stretchers, rolled them up, and sneaking out, dropped them over Blackfriars Bridge into the Thames; water-colours cost less to produce and took up less space, so he adopted them. Mrs. Allingham abandoned oils after a year or two's work in them at the Royal Academy Schools, because she gradually became convinced that she could express herself better in water-colours. But she considered that it was a great advantage to have worked, even for the short time, in the stronger medium. It was this practice in oils that made her for some time (until, indeed, Walker's lessons to her at the Royal Academy) use a good deal of body-colour.

Both artists aspired to obtain the highest rank which then, as now, is open to the water-colourist, namely, membership of The Royal Water-Colour Society, but whilst Birket Foster only attained it in 1860, in his thirty-fifth year, and at his second attempt, Mrs. Allingham followed him in 1875, when only twenty-six, and at her first essay. Both promptly at once gave up a remunerative income in black and white, and having done so, never had cause to regret their decision.

The coincidences do not end even here, for both within a year or two of their election found themselves, the one on the invitation of Mr. Hook, R.A., the other, twenty years later, for reasons we have mentioned, settled near the same village, Witley, in the heart of the country which they have since identified with their names. Here the selection of subjects from the same neighbourhood naturally brought their work still closer together.

Both of them have been attracted to Venice; Mr. Foster again and again, Mrs. Allingham only within the last year or two.

Lastly, few artists have been indulged with so many smiles and so few frowns from the public for which they have catered. Birket Foster considered that he had been almost pampered by the critics, and Mrs. Allingham has never had the slightest cause to complain of her treatment at their hands.

Having dwelt at such length upon the interesting concurrences in their careers, I now pass on to a comparison of their methods of work; and here there are many resemblances, but these are no doubt due to the times in which they lived. Birket Foster found himself, when he commenced, the pupil of a school which had some merits and more demerits. Composition and drawing were still thought of, and before a landscape artist presumed to pose as such, he had to study the laws which governed the former, and to thoroughly imbue himself with a knowledge of the anatomy of what he was about to depict. Mrs. Allingham, as I have pointed out, was also fortunate enough to commence her tuition before the fashion of undergoing this needful apprenticeship died out. But Birket Foster came at the end of a time when landscape was painted in the studio rather than in the field. He went to Nature for suggestions, which he pencilled into note-books in the most facile and learned manner, but content with this he

made his pictures under comfortable conditions at
home.   The fulness of his career, too, came at a
time when Art was booming, and the demand for
his work was such that he could not keep pace
with it.   It is not surprising, therefore, that in the
zenith of his fame his pictures were, in the main,
studio pictures, worked out with a marvellous
facility of invention, but nevertheless just lacking
that vitality which always pervades work done in
the open air and before Nature.

Mrs. Allingham's work at the outset was very
similar to this.   For her subject drawings she
made elaborate preliminary studies from Nature
in colour, but the drawing itself was thought and
carried out in the house.   Fortunately this method
soon became unpalatable to her, and she gradually
came to work more and more directly from Nature,
and when, at Witley, she found her subjects at her
doors, she discontinued once and for ever her
former method.   Since then she has painted every
drawing on the spot during the months that it is
feasible, leaving actual completion for some time,
to enable her to view her work with a fresh eye, and
to study at leisure the final details, such, for instance,
as where the figures shall be grouped, usually
posing, for this purpose, her models in the open air

in her Hampstead garden. Her figures are, however, sometimes culled from careful studies made
in note-books, of which she has an endless supply.
Fastidious to a degree as to the completeness of a
drawing, she lingers long over the finishing touches,
for it is these which she considers make or mar the
whole. Every sort of contrivance she considers to
be legitimate to bring about an effect, save that of
body-colour, which she holds in abhorrence; but
the knife, a hard brush, a pointed stick, a paint
rag, and a sponge are in constant request.

Mrs. Allingham is above all things a fair-weather
painter. She has no pleasure in the storm, whether
of rain or wind. Maybe this avoidance of the
discomforts inseparable from a truthful portrayal
of such conditions indicates the femininity of her
nature. Doubtless it does. But is she to blame?
Her work is framed upon the pleasure that it
affords her, and it is certain that the result is none
the less satisfactory because it only numbers the
sunny hours and the halcyon days.

I ought perhaps to have qualified the expression
"sunny hours," for as a rule she does not affect a
sunshine which casts strong shadows, but rather
its condition when, through a thin veil of cloud, it
suffuses all Nature with an equable light, and allows

local colour to be seen at its best. In drawings which comprise any large amount of floral detail, the leaves, in full sunshine, give off an amount of reflected light that materially lessens the colour value of the flowers, and prevents their being properly distinguished. Mr. Elgood, the painter of flower-gardens *par excellence*, always observes this rule, not only because the effect is so much more satisfactory on paper, but because it is so much easier to paint under this aspect. As regards sky treatment, both he and Mrs. Allingham, it will be noted, confine themselves to the simplest sky effects, feeling that the main interest lies on the ground, where the detail is amply sufficient to warrant the accessories being kept as subservient as possible. For this reason it is that the glories of sunrise and sunset have no place in Mrs. Allingham's work, the hours round mid-day sufficing for her needs.

To the curiously minded concerning her palette, it may be said that it is of the simplest character. Her paint-box is the smallest that will hold her colours in moist cake form, of which none are used save those which she considers to be permanent. It contains cobalt, permanent yellow, aureolin, raw sienna, yellow ochre, cadmium, rose madder, light red, and sepia. She now uses nothing save O.W. (old water-colour) paper. Mrs. Allingham's method of laying on the colour differs from that of Birket Foster, who painted wet and in small touches. Her painting is on the dry side, letting her colours mingle on the paper. As a small bystander once remarked concerning it, "You do mess about a deal."

Mrs. Allingham has been a constant worker for upwards of a quarter of a century, during which time, in addition to contributing to the Royal Society, she has held seven Exhibitions at The Fine Art Society's, each of them averaging some seventy numbers. She has, therefore, upon her own calculation, put forth to the world nearly a thousand drawings. In spite of this, they seldom appear in the sale-room, and when they do they share with Birket Foster's work the unusual distinction of always realising more than the artist received for them.

───────

THE illustrations which adorn this closing chapter have no connection with its subject, but are not on that account altogether out of place; for they are the only ones which are outside the title of the work, two being from Ireland, and two from Venice, and they are associated with two of the main incidents of the artist's life, namely, her marriage, and her only art work abroad.

78. A CABIN AT BALLYSHANNON

From a Water-colour in the possession of the Artist.

Painted 1891.

Ballyshannon is the birthplace of Mr. William Allingham, who married Mrs. Allingham in 1874. It is situated in County Donegal, and was described by him as "an odd, out-of-the way little town on the extreme western verge of Europe; our next neighbours, sunset way, being citizens of the great Republic, which indeed to our imagination seemed little, if at all, farther off than England in the opposite direction. Before it spreads a great ocean, behind stretches many an islanded lake. On the south runs a wavy line of blue mountains, and on the north, over green, rocky hills, rise peaks of a more distant range. The trees hide in glens or cluster near the river; grey rocks and boulders lie scattered about the windy pastures." Here Mr. Allingham was born of the good old stock of one of

Cromwell's settlers, and here he lived until he was two-and-twenty. The drawing now reproduced was made when Mrs. Allingham visited the place with his children after his death in 1889. Many ruined cabins lie around; money is scarce in Donegal, and each year the tenants become fewer, some emigrating, others who have done so sending to their relations to join them. Better times are indeed necessary if the country is not to become a desert.

79. THE FAIRY BRIDGES

From the Water-colour in the possession of the Artist.

Painted 1891.

The Fairy Bridges—a series of natural arches, carved or shaken out of the cliffs, in times long past, by the rollers of the Atlantic—are within a walk of Ballyshannon, and were often visited by Mrs. Allingham during her stay there. Three of them (there are five in all) are seen in the drawing, and a quaint and mythological faith connects them with Elfindom—a faith which every Irishman in the last generation imbibed with his mother's milk, and which is not yet extinct in the lovely crags and glens of Donegal.

The scene is introduced into two of Mr. Allingham's best-known songs; in one, "The Fairies," thus—

> Up the airy mountain,
> Down the rushy glen,
> We daren't go a-hunting
> For fear of little men.
> Down along the rocky shore
> Some make their home,
> They live in crispy pancakes
> Of yellow tide foam.

The only land which separates the wind-swept Fairy Bridges from America is the Slieve-League headland, whose wavy outline is seen in the distance. It, too, finds a place in one of Mr. Allingham's songs, "The Winding Banks of Erne: the Emigrant's Adieu to his Birthplace" (which in ballad form is sung by Erin's children all the world over)—

> Farewell to you, Kildenny lads, and them that pull an oar,
> A lug-sail set, or haul a net, from the Point to Mullaghmore;
> From Killikegs to bold Slieve-League, that ocean mountain steep,
> Six hundred yards in air aloft, six hundred in the deep,
> From Dorran to the Fairy Bridge, and round by Tullen Strand,
> Level and long and white with waves, where gull and curlew
>   stand,
> Head out to sea, when on your lee the breakers you discern!
> Adieu to all the billowy coast, and winding banks of Erne!"

By a curious coincidence Mr. Allingham when here in "the eighties" sent an "Invitation to a Painter"[1]—

O come hither! weeks together let us watch the big Atlantic,
Blue or purple, green or gurly, dark or shining, smooth or frantic;

but the first to come was his own wife.

80. THE CHURCH OF STA. MARIA DELLA SALUTE, VENICE

From the Water-colour in the possession of Mr. C. P. Johnson.

Painted 1901

Mrs. Allingham, after an absence of thirty-three years, visited Italy again in 1901, in company with a fellow-artist, and the following year the Exhibition of the Old Water-Colour Society was rendered additionally interesting by a comparison of her rendering of Venice with that of a fellow lady-member, Miss Clara Montalba, to whose individuality in dealing with it we have before referred.

The drawing of Mrs. Allingham's here reproduced shows Venice in quite an English aspect as regards weather. It is almost a grey day; it certainly is a fresh one, and has nothing in common

[1] *Irish Songs and Poems* (1887), p. 47.

with one which induces the spending of much
time about in a gondola.

In selecting the Salute for one of her principal
illustrations of Venice, Mrs. Allingham has respectfully followed in the footsteps of England's greatest
landscapist, for Turner made it the main object in
his great effort of the Grand Canal, and there are
few of the craft who have failed to limn it again
and again in their story of Venice.

But whilst most people are disposed to regard
it as one of the most beautiful features of the
city, the church has fallen under the ban of
those exponents of architecture that have studied
it carefully.

Mr. Ruskin classified it under the heading of
"Grotesque Renaissance," although he admitted
that its position, size, and general proportions
rendered it impressive. Its proportions were
good, but its graceful effect was due to the in-
equality in the size of its cupolas and the pretty
grouping of the campaniles behind them. But
he qualified his praise by an opinion that the
proportions of buildings have nothing whatever
to do with the style or general merits of their
architecture, for an artist trained in the worst
schools, and utterly devoid of all meaning and

purpose in his work, may yet have such a natural gift of massing or grouping as will render all his structures effective when seen from a distance. Such a gift was very general with the late Italian builders, so that many of the most contemptible edifices in the country have a good stage effect so long as we do not approach them. The Church of the Salute is much assisted by the beautiful flight of steps in front of it down to the Canal, and its façade is rich and beautiful of its kind. What raised the anger of Ruskin was the disguise of the buttresses under the form of colossal scrolls, the buttresses themselves being originally a hypocrisy, for the cupola is of timber, and therefore needs none.

81. A FRUIT STALL, VENICE

From the Drawing, the property of Mr. C. P. Johnson.

Painted 1902.

A lover of gardens and their produce, such as Mrs. Allingham is, could not visit Venice without being captivated by the wealth of colour which Nature has lavished upon the contents of the Venetian fruit stalls. Even the most indifferent, when they get into meridional parts, cannot be

insensible to the luscious hues which the fruit
baskets display. To look out of the window of
one's hotel on an Italian lake-side at dawn and see
the boats coming from all quarters of the lake
laden with the luscious tomatoes, plums, and other
fruits, is not among the least of the delights of a
sojourn there. Mrs. Allingham's drawing bears
upon its face evidences that it is a literal translation
of the scene. We have none of the introduction
of stage accessories in the way of secchios and
other studio belongings which find a place in
most of the Venetian output of this character.
She has evidently delighted in the mysteries of
the tones of the wicker baskets, for we recognise
in them traces of the skill she achieves in England
in the delineation of similar surfaces on her tiled
roofs. Her figure, too, has nothing of the studio
model in it. This black-haired girl is a new type
for her, but it is a faithful transcript of the original,
and not one of the robust beauties which one is
accustomed to in the pictures of Van Haanen and
his followers. The stall itself was located somewhere between the Campo San Stefano and the
Rialto.

With these illustrations of Mrs. Allingham's painting elsewhere than in England our tale is told. We trust that this digression, which appeared to be necessary if a complete survey of the artist's lifework up to the present time was to be portrayed, will not be deemed to have appreciably affected the appropriateness of the title to the volume, nor invalidated the claim that we have made as to her work having most felicitously represented the fairest aspects of English life and landscape—English life, whether of peer, commoner, or peasant, passed under its healthiest and happiest conditions, and English landscape under spring and summer skies and dressed in its most beauteous array of flower and foliage—an England of which we may to-day be as proud as were those who lived when the immortal lines concerning it were penned :—

> This royal throne of kings, this sceptred isle,
> This earth of majesty, this seat of Mars,
> This other Eden, demi-paradise ;
> This fortress built by Nature for herself
> Against infection and the hand of war ;
> This happy breed of men, this little world ;
> This precious stone set in the silver sea,
> Which serves it in the office of a wall,
> Or as a moat defensive to a house,

Against the envy of less happier lands ;
This blessed plot, this earth, this realm, this England,
This nurse, this teeming womb of royal kings,
This land of such dear souls, this dear dear land,
Dear for reputation through the world ;—
England, bound in with the triumphant sea,
Whose rocky shore beats back the envious siege
Of watery Neptune.

THE END